DETERMINANTS AND CONSEQUENCES OF INTERNAL MIGRATION IN INDIA

DETERMINANTS AND CONSEQUENCES OF INTERNAL MIGRATION IN INDIA

Studies in Bihar, Kerala and Uttar Pradesh

A. S. OBERAI

PRADHAN H. PRASAD

and

M. G. SARDANA

DELHI
OXFORD UNIVERSITY PRESS
BOMBAY CALCUTTA MADRAS
1989

Oxford University Press, Walton Street, Oxford OX2 6DP

NEW YORK TORONTO
DELHI BOMBAY CALCUTTA MADRAS KARACHI
PETALING JAYA SINGAPORE HONG KONG TOKYO
NAIROBI DAR ES SALAAM
MELBOURNE AUCKLAND
and associates in
BERLIN IBADAN

Phototypeset by Spantech Publishers Pvt Ltd, New Delhi 110060
Printed by Rekha Printers (P) Ltd, New Delhi 110020
and published by S. K. Mookerjee, Oxford University Press
YMCA Library Building, Jai Singh Road, New Delhi 110001

NOTE

Founded in 1974, the Labour and Population Team for Asia and the Pacific (LAPTAP) is responsible for all population-related activities of the International Labour Organization (ILO) in the region. The two main thrusts of the LAPTAP programme are:

Introduction of population education/family welfare programmes as part of labour welfare, occupational health, workers' education and other activities in the industrial sector and other work-related institutions;

Promotion of consideration of demographic factors in all aspects of development planning, with emphasis on employment and integration of population, human resources and development planning.

Within this framework LAPTAP promotes the participation of ILO's tripartite constituents—labour administrations, employers and workers—and other labour sector organizations in population activities; technically supports a large number of externally-funded (mainly UNFPA-funded) country projects; provides advisory services in setting up and implementing population projects/programmes; undertakes and commissions research studies relevant to its programmes; conducts and assists in the organization of seminars, workshops, international fellowship programmes and other training activities at various levels.

The present study was prepared for the ILO's Labour and Population team for Asia and the Pacific (LAPTAP) as part of a technical co-operation project executed in collaboration with the Central Statistical Organization (CSO), Ministry of Planning, Govt of India, with the financial support of the United Nations Population Fund (UNPF).

FOREWORD

Migration, especially rural-urban migration, is often viewed with alarm and blamed for the many problems faced by developing countries. However, the overcrowding and poor quality of life in cities is as much a reflection of rapid population growth as of the relentless drift away from the countryside. It is now widely realized that urbanization is inevitable and that population movements are integral features of the process of growth. To stop migration may be tantamount to damming one of the mainsprings of growth. It is therefore necessary to devote much more attention to channelizing the propensity to migrate so that the resulting process of population redistribution leads to better living standards for all. This in turn will require the use of an appropriate mix of policy instruments to achieve the goals of each country.

The authors of this volume pose this issue very clearly when they argue that 'a clear and thorough understanding of migration, interwoven as it is in the development process, is essential for the formulation of appropriate migration-influencing policies'. A number of factors are considered and their interrelations with migration systematically analysed. These include factors such as education, employment, technology and productivity, remittance flows and expenditure patterns, and housing and civic amenities. There are a number of important conclusions reached by the authors and these have wider policy implications. For example, the authors conclude that rural-urban migration is often a desperate survival strategy and it would not be humane to attempt to stop it. Their analysis also shows that migration to urban areas generates some benefits for the rural areas in terms of the inflow of remittances and their investment in raising productivity and incomes. These positive benefits, they argue, should not be overlooked while attempting to formulate population distribution policies.

This volume is the outcome of a collaborative research effort undertaken by the ILO and the Central Statistical Organization, Government of India, under a UNFPA funded country technical co-operation project IND/81/PO2: 'Policy Research on Internal

Migration in India'. We are grateful to the United Nations Population Fund for its financial support. We take pleasure in placing this volume before a wider audience in India and in other countries as we believe it contributes to a better understanding of the complex phenomenon of migration which has much impact on the lives of people in the Asia and Pacific region.

Bangkok, June 1989

D. L. KHANNA

Director

ILO Labour and Population Team for

Asia and the Pacific (LAPTAP)

PREFACE

Migration and urbanization act as a catalyst for economic and social advance. This was amply demonstrated by the Ludhiana study carried out by the ILO in collaboration with the Department of Economics, Punjabi University, Patiala, during 1977 with the financial support of UNFPA. (A. S. Oberai and H. K. Manmohan Singh, 1983, *Causes and consequences of internal migration: A study in the Indian Punjab*, Oxford University Press, New Delhi.) The Ludhiana study had therefore suggested that the real challenge to policy is not to devise measures to stop migration but to develop feasible policy instruments to influence the direction and magnitude of migration flows in order to harness the positive effects of migration and to mitigate the negative consequences and social disparities resulting from a disorderly population distribution.

But since Punjab is a relatively more developed state and the pattern of migration and its implications are likely to be different from those in other less developed areas in India, it was suggested by the Advisory Committee, which was specially set up to advise and assist in the implementation of the Punjab study, that there is a need to undertake two or three more case studies, more or less on lines similar to the Ludhiana case study, to provide comparable results under different sets of situations. The Government of India took a keen interest in this suggestion and with the assistance of the ILO secured funding from UNFPA for the technical co-operation project IND/81/PO2. The project activities involved case studies in the States of Bihar, Kerala and Uttar Pradesh. These three states were selected for case studies in consultation with the Office of the Registrar-General, and after carefully examining the migration flows from the 1971 Census. The project was implemented by the Central Statistical Organization (CSO), Department of Statistics, Ministry of Planning, with technical assistance from the ILO. The Director-General, CSO, was the Project Director and had the main responsibility for the successful completion of the project.

An advisory committee of distinguished academics and government officials was set up under the chairmanship of the Director-General,

CSO, to advise and assist in the execution of the project. The committee included, among others, representatives of the Department of Town and Country Planning, Department of Family Welfare, Planning Commission, Office of the Registrar-General of India, and National Sample Survey Organization (NSSO). We are extremely grateful to members of the committee for their constructive and helpful suggestions.

The case studies in Bihar, Kerala and Uttar Pradesh were carried out by A. N. Sinha Institute of Social Sciences (ANSISS), Patna; Kerala Statistical Institute (KSI), Trivandrum; and Operations Research Group (ORG), Baroda, respectively. Each of these institutes had done preliminary analysis of data and had prepared draft reports. We owe a deep sense of gratitude to these local institutes for their excellent work. Special thanks are also due to Dr A. N. Sharma (ANSISS), and Dr N. T. Mathew (KSI), and Dr M. E. Khan and Mr R. B. Gupta (ORG) for their help and co-operation.

The work on comparative analysis and preparation of the consolidated report was partly undertaken in Geneva. We wish to acknowledge programming and research assistance received from Mr P. Cornu, Dr P. P. Ghosh, Dr A. N. Sharma, Mr M. R. Balakrishnan, Mr Kailash Prasad, Ms Alicia Cackley and Ms Suja Rishikesh.

The present study reports the major findings of the migration surveys carried out in the states of Bihar, Kerala and Uttar Pradesh. It complements the Punjab Migration Study and provides a reasonably good picture of the process of migration and its likely consequences in a developing country, such as India. Many of the conclusions drawn in the Punjab study are reinforced by the data gathered in the other three states. The present study, for example, also suggests that migration can generate substantial benefits not only for migrants themselves but also for areas of origin and destination. It therefore also cautions policy-makers against adopting anti-migration policies without adequately examining the causes and consequences of migration in a particular context. An interesting finding of the present study is, however, that the lower the level of rural development in general and of infrastructural development in particular, the smaller the gains from migration. The finding of the present study that many employed persons also migrate to the cities suggests that the provision of employment opportunities in rural areas are unlikely to slow down migration unless differentials in income and living conditions are reduced between rural and urban areas.

A number of persons have helped in one way or another in completing the present study. We are especially grateful to J. Krishnamurty, Ashish Bose, K. M. Bashir and Ghazi Farooq for their useful comments and criticisms on survey and research design and on the earlier drafts of the chapters. We are also grateful to the Director and staff of the ILO, Area Office, New Delhi, for their valuable assistance, and to Mr Jalaluddin Ahmed, Mr P. A. Chakravarty and Mrs Divjoti Datta for their help during the course of the study. Special thanks are also due to Ms H. Najaf and Mrs A. Eggleston, who painstakingly, but cheerfully, typed several successive drafts of the manuscript.

We would also like to express our gratitude to the United Nations Population Fund (UNFPA) for its support of this work.

Needless to say, the contents of this study represent our own positions, and not necessarily that of UNFPA or those of the organizations to which we belong. The responsibility for any errors or shortcomings must therefore rest solely on us, as authors.

June 1989   A. S. Oberai
                                                  Pradhan H. Prasad
                                                      M. G. Sardana

CONTENTS

CHAPTER 1

INTRODUCTION

Urbanization and migration have come to be regarded as the most pressing population problems in almost all the developing countries, even more pressing than high fertility and natural population growth rates (United Nations, 1985). Until 1970, the size of the urban population in the developed world was larger than that in the developing world, but now the majority of the world's urban population lives in developing countries. According to a recent UN estimate, the world's urban population had reached 1,983 million in 1985, of which about three-fifths lived in the less developed regions of the world. By the year 2000, it is predicted that more than two-thirds of the 2,854 million urban dwellers of the world will reside in the less developed regions (United Nations, 1987).

It is felt in some quarters that the huge influx of population to urban centres from rural areas is responsible for the declining quality of urban life in developing countries. Scanty housing, inadequate water and power supply, poor sanitation, and shortage of transport and other civic amenities are attributed largely to rural-urban migration. It is often alleged that the rural areas are also adversely affected by this process because migration remains, by and large, selective, and therefore draws away the more dynamic members of rural society. On the other hand, there is some evidence that rural-urban migration is not always detrimental to development, particularly in poor countries with a low level of urbanization (Oberai and Singh, 1983). Migration which tends to integrate rural and urban areas increasingly through the flow of labour, capital and information may indeed positively influence investment and technological development. In a labour surplus economy like India, rural-urban migration on a sufficient scale may also reduce under-employment and disguised unemployment in the rural areas, improve income distribution through remittances, and weaken the traditional, outmoded, semi-feudal agrarian structure.

A large volume of literature has grown up around these issues in

Table 1.1: Key statistics on urbanization in India, 1901–81

Census	Number of towns	Total population (million)	Urban population (million)	Population in towns above 20,000 (million)	Level of urbanization (%)	Intercensal annual growth rate		Difference between urban and rural growth rates (7) – (8)
						Urban population	Rural population	
(1)	(2)	(3)	(4)	(5)	(6)	(7)	(8)	(9)
1901	1 917	238.4	25.8	13.0	10.8	—	—	—
1911	1 909	252.1	25.9	13.5	10.3	0.04	0.62	– 0.58
1921	2 047	251.3	28.1	15.1	11.2	0.82	– 0.13	0.95
1931	2 219	279.0	33.4	18.9	12.0	1.73	0.96	0.77
1941	2 424	318.7	44.1	27.8	13.8	2.78	1.12	1.66
1951	3 059	361.1	62.4	42.5	17.3	3.47	0.84	2.63
1961	2 699	439.2	78.9	60.4	18.0	2.35	1.87	0.48
1971	3 126	548.2	109.1	88.0	19.9	3.21	1.98	1.23
1981	3 303	665.3	157.7	135.8	23.7	3.83	1.76	2.07

Source: Adapted from Visaria and Kothari (1985), table 1.

recent years. Some of the views put forward have been in the nature of hypotheses, not yet fully supported by empirical results, while there have been some empirical findings whose theoretical basis has not yet been fully developed. But a proper understanding of these issues is important for the formulation of policy in the developing countries. The major question being asked is whether rural-urban migration should be regulated, drastically reduced or stopped altogether by direct state intervention, or whether only the negative aspects of such migration should be tackled. In order to answer such questions, a scientific and area-specific study of internal migration is required. It is with this end in view that the present study attempts to answer some of these questions in the context of India, the second most populous country of the world.

1.1 *Urbanization and migration in India*

A little less than one-quarter of the total population of India is urban, but the absolute size of the urban population has grown to about 160 million (1981 census); hence the phenomenon assumes importance. India has experienced a steady, though slow, growth in urbanization since 1911—its urban population increased from about 10 per cent in 1911 to 24 per cent in 1981 (table 1.1). The growth of the urban population has occurred through the addition of new towns, the enlargement of existing towns, the natural increase in population, and rural-urban migration. Net rural-urban migration accounted for about one-fifth of total urban growth during 1961–71 and 1971–81 (table 1.2).

Table 1.3 shows that though about two-thirds of the total migration stream in 1981 is accounted for by rural-rural migration, this form of migration has declined steadily since the 1961 census, whereas rural-urban migration has shown an increase. Much of the census-defined migration is accounted for by traditional migration streams—seasonal, circular or marital. The most important rural-rural migratory flows are dominated by short-distance (within district) migration, and within that female migrants dominate. The predominant form of migration in India is thus rural-rural female migration, most of which is marriage migration (Skeldon, 1986).

However, though in terms of magnitude rural-urban migration accounts for only about one-sixth of the total migration stream in India (1981 census), it assumes great importance both because it is usually influenced by economic considerations and because of its

Table 1.2: Components of urban growth, India, 1961–71 and 1971–81

Component	1961–71		1971–81*	
	Number (million)	%	Number (million)	%
Absolute increase	30.2	100.0	49.9	100.0
Net reclassification of localities from rural to urban	4.5	14.9	6.7	13.4
Net rural-urban migration	6.3	20.9	9.8	19.6
Natural increase (i) of initial urban population	18.8	62.3	24.5	49.1
(ii) of intercensal migrants (net figure)	0.7	2.3	1.1	2.2
Residual (including errors and changes in boundaries)	−0.1	−0.3	7.8	15.6

* Excluding Assam.
Source: Adapted from Visaria and Kothari (1985), table 19.

Table 1.3: Rural-urban composition of migrants in India

(in millions)

Census (1)	R–R (2)	R–U (3)	U–R (4)	U–U (5)	Unclassified (6)	Total (7)
1961	99.1 (73.2)	19.6 (14.5)	4.8 (3.5)	10.8 (8.0)	1.0 (0.7)	135.3 (99.9)
1971	113.0 (70.6)	23.7 (14.8)	7.9 (4.9)	14.0 (8.7)	1.5 (0.9)	160.1 (99.9)
1981	128.1 (65.3)	34.2 (17.4)	11.7 (6.0)	21.8 (11.1)	0.5 (0.2)	196.3 (100.0)

Note: Numbers in parentheses are breakdowns of shares by pattern (%).
1981 data do not include the State of Assam.
Source: Makoto Kojima (1981).

contribution to the process of urbanization and development.

The size of India's urban population is expected to increase from about 160 million in 1981 to about 320 million in 2001. The urban proportion of the total population would also increase from 23.7 per cent in 1981 to about 32 per cent in 2001 (Mohan, 1985). Further, the proportion of the urban population living in large cities will increase due both to rural-urban migration and to natural growth. This would

call for a massive increase in resources to cope with the demand for
housing and other social services in urban areas, particularly in large
cities (Government of India, Planning Commission, 1983; National
Institute of Urban Affairs, 1988).

1.2 *Background and objectives of the study*

There is a growing interest in India in devising programmes for
changing or controlling migratory flows. India's Sixth Plan document
makes a graphic reference to the impending peril of a 'breakdown'
of 'all civic services', and strongly recommends 'drastic measures' to
restrict 'the growth of population in the larger urban conglomerates'
(Government of India, Planning Commission, 1978, pp. 243–44).
The Seventh Plan document reiterates similar concerns.

Many policies have already been introduced to regulate migration.
These include dispersal of industries and balanced regional development, establishment of heavy industries (like steel) in new townships,
land development schemes and opening up of new agricultural areas.
However, the available evidence suggests that most such policies
have had limited success so far; they have also tended to have unanti-
cipated side effects, while using up considerable scarce financial and
physical resources, as in the case of many resettlement programmes
and urban dispersal schemes. One reason why population distribution
policies have been largely unsuccessful is that they have often been
formulated without adequate knowledge of the causes and consequences of migration; hence little is known about whether the existing
policies are in fact justified and appropriate.

It was in that practical context that at the beginning of 1977, the
ILO initiated a major survey-based study of population mobility
and economic change in the Ludhiana district in the Indian Punjab.
The main focus of this study was the analysis of interaction between
rural-urban migration and socio-economic change, emphasising the
functions of migration in the transformation of rural and urban
economies and its effects on production, agricultural productivity,
technological change (through transfer of physical and human
capital), population growth, the structure and level of employment
and unemployment, and income distribution between and within
rural and urban areas.

The Punjab study provided a reasonably good picture of the process
of internal migration and its role in rural and urban development.
But the Punjab is a relatively developed state, and the pattern of

migration and its implications are likely to be different from those in other less developed areas. It was, therefore, considered desirable to cover other states in order to provide comparable models under different sets of situations for deriving more meaningful conclusions. Accordingly, three other states which are at various stages of socio-economic development—Bihar, Kerala and Uttar Pradesh—were selected for the purposes of this study. Taken together, the present study and the Punjab study provide a better understanding of the process of migration and its policy implications in a large, heterogeneous country like India.

Within this framework, a number of questions, which have a direct impact on the design of policy, have been examined.[1] These include:

(i) What are the socio-economic characteristics of migrants?

(ii) What is the impact of migration on the demographic structure of the migrant households?

(iii) Does out-migration from rural to urban areas result in improvement in the quality of life and economy of the rural areas because of:

   (a) reduction in unemployment and disguised unemployment in a labour surplus situation and, therefore, improvement in income distribution,

   (b) remittances which not only improve income distribution but also result in technological development and increases in production, and

   (c) information and resource inflow through return-migrants?

(iv) How quickly and to what extent are migrants absorbed into the urban labour market?

(v) Are migrants from the rural areas the main cause of rising levels of unemployment in the urban areas?

(vi) Do migrants lack access to social services in urban areas?

(vii) What are the policy implications of different types of migration flows for rural and urban development?

The three states selected for the present study—Bihar, Kerala and Uttar Pradesh—are among the less developed states in India. However, they differ widely among themselves in terms of demographic, social and economic characteristics. While Bihar and Uttar

[1] For a definition of different types of migrants (out-migrant, in-migrant or return-migrant) see section 1.4.

Pradesh are the most populous states of India, having about one-tenth and one-sixth of the population of the country respectively, Kerala accounts for only 3.8 per cent of the population of India (table 1.4). All three states have low urbanization levels compared with the national level, but the level of urbanization in Bihar is much lower than in the other two states—in fact, Bihar is among the least urbanized states of India. While all three states are more densely populated than India as a whole, Kerala has the highest population density in the country. Nearly 30 per cent of the population participates in economic activities in Bihar and Uttar Pradesh, but in Kerala the figure is somewhat lower (about 27 per cent). However, the proportion of female workers is considerably higher in Kerala than in either Bihar or Uttar Pradesh. This higher participation of women in economic activities in Kerala is due to the higher levels of social awareness and education in the state. Kerala has the highest level of literacy in India, whereas Bihar and Uttar Pradesh are among the least literate states in the country. Not only this, but in regard to many other types of social infrastructure, Kerala is the foremost state of India: it has a good system of medical care, the lowest infant mortality rate, and one of the lowest population growth rates in the country. Bihar and Uttar Pradesh, on the other hand, are among the most backward states in this regard.

In terms of economic development, though all three states are among the less developed states of India, they represent the three levels of development. Among the major states of India, Bihar is at the bottom in terms of economic development. In 1981–82 per capita income in Bihar was the lowest (Rs 995) in India, about 45 per cent less than the national average (Rs 1,750). Per capita income in Uttar Pradesh was also lower than the national average. Both Bihar and Uttar Pradesh have a very high percentage of workers dependent on agriculture—much higher than even the national average—but growth of agricultural output is higher in Uttar Pradesh than in Bihar (table 1.4). The percentage of workers engaged in industry is also lower in Bihar than in the other two states selected.

Kerala is much less dependent on agriculture than the other two states. In Kerala fisheries and other primary activities are also important; the state also has a much higher percentage of workers engaged in industry than either Bihar or Uttar Pradesh.

Presumably because of low land-man ratios and low levels of economic development, both of which have hindered the expansion

**Table 1.4: Some basic statistics relating to
Bihar, Kerala, Uttar Pradesh and India, 1981**

	Bihar	Kerala	Uttar Pradesh	India
Percentage of India's population	10.3	3.8	16.5	100
Percentage of urban population	11.3	18.7	17.8	23.3
Population per sq.km	402	655	377	216
Percentage of male workers to population	30.1	26.7	29.3	33.5
Percentage of female workers to total workers	14.8	24.3	8.7	20.2
Percentage of workers in agriculture	79.1	41.3	74.5	66.5
Percentage of workers in industry	6.3	16.1	10.4	11.3
Percentage of literate population	26.2	70.42	27.2	36.2
Percentage net area irrigated	35.5	10.9	38.5	27.7
Per capita annual income at current prices 1981–82	995	NA	1 303	1 750
Annual compound rate of growth of agricultural production 1969–70 to 1983–84	0.49	0.23	3.19	3.0

Sources: Census 1981, Paper 2 of 1983; *State domestic product*, Central Statistical
Organization (CSO); *Report on prices for kharif crops 1985–86 season*,
Commission of Agricultural Costs and Prices, Government of India
(mimeograph), 1986, p. 69; *Statistical Abstract*, 1984.

of employment opportunities, all three states have a high rate of
out-migration. Between 1951 and 1971, Bihar, Kerala and Uttar
Pradesh were the states which lost the most population by migration
(Bhande and Kanitkar, 1980). A large number of people from these
states have migrated to other parts of the country. From Kerala,
substantial numbers have crossed the national boundaries, mainly
to Gulf countries. The social and economic implications of this
migration from Kerala are therefore likely to be different from those
of the other two states selected for the study.

1.3 *Selection of study areas*

When analysing the causes and implications of migration for rural
and urban development, it is essential to study both the sending and
the receiving areas. Accordingly, in this study both an urban house-

hold survey and a rural household survey were carried out in the three selected states. In each state two urban centres (except in Uttar Pradesh, where there was only one) with substantial in-migration and two rural centres with substantial out-migration were chosen.

In Bihar, the two urban centres selected were Muzaffarpur and Bokaro Steel City. Muzaffarpur, situated on the plains of North Bihar, with a population of 190,000 in 1981, owes its size and importance to the fact that it is a large commercial and trading centre, an important administrative headquarters and a centre for a good number of educational institutions in the state. Bokaro Steel City, on the other hand, located in the mineral-rich Chhota Nagpur region of South Bihar (where a number of large public and private sector enterprises are also located), is an important industrial town. Between 1971 and 1981, the population of Bokaro increased from 94,000 to 224,000 (one of the highest growth rates of all the towns in India).

As regards the rural centres, Saran in North Bihar and Singhbhum in the Chhota Nagpur plateau were chosen. Of these two, Saran is known to be an area of high out-migration whereas Singhbhum was chosen mainly to study the migration among tribal people, who constitute about half the population of the district. The choice also ensured that the two rural centres chosen were quite close to the two urban centres—Saran close to Muzaffarpur and Singhbhum close to Bokaro. Saran is essentially a rural district dependent almost entirely on cultivation—the district is more rural and more densely populated than the rest of the state. The relatively higher level of mobility among the district's male population, which is probably caused by its high population density and backward agriculture, is reflected in the higher sex ratio in the district—1,041 women per 1,000 men as against 946 for the state. Singhbhum is one of the most mineral-rich districts in India, and because of this it contains some important industries, including the steel plant at Jamshedpur, its most important town. The level of urbanization of the district is, consequently, much higher (32 per cent) than that of Bihar as a whole.

In Kerala, the two urban centres chosen were the two most populous cities in the state. Trivandrum is the seat of the state government and Cochin in Ernakulam district is a centre of industrial and commercial activities. The two rural centres chosen were the rural parts of Trivandrum and Ernakulam districts—the rural areas surrounding the two urban centres selected. In the district of Trivandrum 75 per cent of the population lives in rural areas. The density of population is much higher (1,184 persons per square kilometre) than the state average of 654. Ernakulam district has the highest degree of urbanization in the state – 40 per cent as against the state average of only 19 per cent. The average density of population is also very high (1,053 persons per square kilometre). The district has a large industrial base, mostly concentrated in Cochin and its peripheral areas; hence there has been a rapid increase in commercial and banking activities.

In Uttar Pradesh, Kanpur City was selected as the urban centre and the adjoining rural areas—the rural part of Kanpur district—as one of the rural centres. The other rural centre selected was the hilly district of Almora, as it has been observed that a sizeable number of people from hilly areas migrate to the plains in search of employment. The impact of such migration is well reflected in the sex ratio for the district—Almora had as many as 1,081 females for every 1,000 males in 1981, as against 886 for the state as a whole. Kanpur City, with a population of 1.69 million in 1981, is one of India's major industrial cities.

1.4 *Survey and sample design*

As noted earlier, the study is based on the primary data collected in comprehensive surveys conducted in the above-mentioned rural and urban areas of the three states. The rural surveys concentrated on out-migration and to a lesser extent on return- and in-migration, while the urban surveys focused on in-migration. In the study of Kerala where out-migration to foreign countries, particularly to Gulf countries, is an important phenomenon, this issue has also received some attention.

A significant number of non-migrant households were also selected in each area to serve as a comparison group. The initial plan was to have a sample size of about 1,000 households from each of the rural and urban areas (except Kanpur, where the sample size was to be 2,000) to cover all types of migrant and non-migrant households. The number of different types of households in rural and urban areas was planned as follows:

Rural: out-migrant, 800; in-migrant, 200; return-migrant, 200; non-migrant, 800.

Urban: in-migrant, 800; out-migrant, 200; return-migrant, 200; non-migrant, 800.

For identification of the different types of households, the following definitions were used:

Out-migrant households: An out-migrant household was defined as one from which at least one person who was previously a member of the household had left since 1971 to live or work elsewhere. Women who out-migrated for marriage and children below 10 years of age at the time of migration were excluded. Since commuters retain their residence, they were also excluded.

In-migrant households: An in-migrant household was defined as one which contained at least one person who was not born in his/her present place of residence, but had in-migrated since 1971. Wives who had in-migrated because of marriage and children below 10 years of age at the time of in-migration were excluded.

Return-migrant households: A return-migrant household was defined as one which contained at least one person who had lived away, either working or looking for work or studying, for at least six months, and had returned since 1971, irrespective of when he/she had out-migrated.

Non-migrant households: A household which did not fall into any one of the above categories was classified as a non-migrant household.

(a) RURAL SAMPLE

In the rural areas, the sampling was carried out in three stages— blocks, villages and households.[2]

(i) SELECTION OF BLOCKS

Three blocks from each of the districts in the three states were selected, keeping in view the extent of the migrant population in the blocks. However, in Kerala, the three blocks surrounding each town (not adjoining) were selected.

(ii) SELECTION OF VILLAGES

Since the villages closest to the towns are more likely to contain people who commute rather than change their residence, it seemed more appropriate to concentrate on villages more than 15 kilometres away from the nearest town (10 kilometres in the case of hilly areas like Almora). Hence, a list of all such villages was prepared for each block and five villages were selected randomly from each list. The

---

[2] A block is a geographical area below the district level comprising a group of about 100 villages.

number of villages was increased (again selected at random) if the listing of households in any block did not give a sufficient number of out-migrant households. Thus, the total number of villages surveyed was 35 in Bihar—15 in Saran and 20 in Singhbhum districts—and 47 in Uttar Pradesh—23 in Almora and 24 in Kanpur districts. In Kerala, four *panchayats* with a concentration of migrant households were selected from each block.[3]

(iii) SELECTION OF HOUSEHOLDS

Initially, it was planned to select the allocated number of households in each rural centre from the selected villages on a random basis. However, experience showed that random sampling procedures would not generate adequate numbers of the different types of migrant households, which was necessary, given the focus and diagnostic nature of the present study. In order to ensure a sufficiently large number of each category of migrant household, all the households in the selected villages were listed on a census basis and then categorized into different types of migrant households. The village lists were then merged and a consolidated list prepared for each block. Wherever possible, the sample of households was allotted equally between the blocks. The list of all the households thus finally prepared was used as a sampling frame. If the listing of households did not provide an adequate number of return-migrant and/or in-migrant households, the shortfall was made up by a corresponding increase in the number of out-migrant households, which were the main focus of the study in the rural areas.

In each category, households were selected on the basis of circular systematic sampling with a random start. But if in a given migrant category there were just adequate or less than adequate households for the sample size, all the households in that category were taken.

In Kerala, the households to be listed (2,000 from each centre) were initially distributed equally among the three blocks. The number of households allotted to each block was then distributed equally among the four *panchayats* and in the *panchayat* among four wards selected at random. The lists of households from the wards in each *panchayat* were pooled and examined to ensure that a sufficient

[3] A panchayat is a group of households below the block level generally comprising a population of 20,000.

number of households belonging to each category of migrant household was available. If the number was insufficient for any category, additional households were listed in wards with a concentration of migrant households of that category to make up the shortfall.

(b) URBAN SAMPLE

The selection of the sample in the urban areas was done in two stages—selection of localities and selection of households.

(i) SELECTION OF LOCALITIES

The selection of localities in Bihar and Uttar Pradesh was done with the help of sampling frames used by the National Sample Survey Organization (NSSO), which first divides each urban area into Investigator Units (IU) and then subdivides each IU into Enumeration Blocks (EB). On the basis of discussions with NSSO officials and other knowledgeable persons with regard to the extent of the migrant population in different IUs, they were stratified and a sample of six IUs from Kanpur and three each from the two urban areas in Bihar were undertaken. From each selected IU, five enumeration blocks (EB) were selected randomly. After listing the households, however, the required number of a particular category of migrant household sometimes fell short; in this case the listing was extended to a few more blocks, again selected at random. Altogether 32 blocks from six IUs from Kanpur, 16 blocks from three IUs from Muzaffarpur and 15 blocks from three IUs from Bokaro were taken for sampling. For selecting localities in the urban areas of Kerala, municipal wards were used instead of NSSO sampling frames.

(ii) SELECTION OF HOUSEHOLDS

In each selected EB (ward in the case of Kerala), the listing of households was undertaken on a census basis with their migration status also noted, and then a merged list was prepared for each IU. The requisite sample size for each migrant category in an IU was worked out on the basis of proportional allocation. In each category, a circular systematic sample of households was drawn with a random start. Any shortfall in the sample size of out-migrant and/or return-migrant households in an urban survey was made up by a corresponding increase in the sample of in-migrant households.

The details of the sample size selected in each centre/state are presented in table 1.5.

The field surveys were carried out during 1984–85. In Bihar the field work lasted from June 1984 to February 1985; in Kerala from July 1984 to March 1985, and in Uttar Pradesh from August to December 1984.

Table 1.5: Distribution of selected households by migration status

Type of household	Bihar		Kerala		Uttar Pradesh	
	Rural	*Urban*	*Rural*	*Urban*	*Rural*	*Urban*
Out-migrant	961	—	721	—	793	—
In-migrant	—	848	—	662	—	827
Return-migrant	200	—	249	200*	198	—
Non-migrant	883	1 171	1 020	1 045	1 009	1 190
Total	2 044	2 019	1 990	1 907	2 000	2 017

* Excluded from the analysis for the preparation of this report.

CHAPTER 2

THEORETICAL FORMULATION

A scientific study involves a theoretical formulation which gives rise to hypotheses which are then tested with reference to facts. It often happens that the hypotheses are modified as a consequence of empirical findings, tested again, and thereafter result in final generalizations about the issues under study. A theoretical formulation is therefore a pre-condition for any valid empirical study. However, a theoretical formulation cannot remain independent of time and space. In the present case, while attempting a theoretical formulation on migration, we are basically concerned with the current situation in India. India is a developing economy characterised by a predominance of primary activities (mainly agriculture), surplus labour supply, and a process of uneven regional development where large rural areas have been caught up in the quagmire of non-development (Prasad, 1986, 1987).

The basis for a theoretical formulation of the present study of internal migration is in terms of the Hicksian indifference analysis. According to this analysis, a person's level of satisfaction (or utility) is a function of leisure and income; the person can obtain income either by sacrificing leisure (and obtaining wage income) or by having productive assets (a source of non-wage income) or both. In the diagram below income is measured on Y-axis and leisure on X-axis. The person's leisure is fixed and given, which is equal to OM. The labour supply is, therefore, measured as OM minus leisure, i.e. in the direction from M towards O. Let us assume that a person has a productive asset (in rural India, usually cultivable land), the income from which as a function of labour input is defined by the curve MQS. Let us assume that the existing wage rate is given by OA divided by OM, that is the slope of AM. The person, therefore, can obtain a non-wage income equal to PM by employing labour from outside and incurring a labour cost RN = QN-PM. The income possibility curve for the person is therefore defined by BPM. Here BP is parallel to AM.

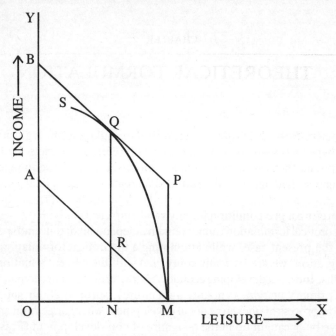

If the person's indifference curve (between leisure and income) is tangential to BP at point Q, the person is enjoying an income of NQ and leisure of ON. It is immaterial whether he is a self-employed person or an employer in the context of his productive assets and working for others at the existing wage rate. In such a case, the person may be tempted to out-migrate if the rate of earning per unit of time is higher elsewhere than the existing wage rate where the asset is located (the assumption is that the productive asset is mobile only at a loss). The situation will be similar even if the point of tangency is between Q and P. Obviously this situation normally refers to a high per capita productive asset. In other words, the size of family dependent on the person is low. It is a well-known dictum that, *ceteris paribus*, a person's preference for income increases as the size of dependent family increases. In such a case out-migration will increase employment and income and improve income distribution in the area of origin. The only exception to this will be the case where the per capita asset of the person is so high that the point of tangency originally would have been at point P. The out-migrant in this case would be a voluntarily unemployed person.

The other situation may be where the point of tangency is between B and Q. In a surplus labour situation, however, the income possibility curve for the person may be MQS and the point of tangency may therefore be between Q and S, giving rise to dualism in Indian agriculture (maximum or near maximum value of gross output per unit of land) (Sen, 1962). Obviously the per capita asset in this case is so low that it is not sufficient to provide full employment to the person. In such a situation the person may migrate even if the earning rate at the place of destination is no higher, if the possibility of employment is greater than at the place of origin. Those who have no productive assets will be in a similar situation.

Where a person possesses productive assets (mostly cultivable land in rural India), the transfer of such assets from one area to another cannot normally be made without substantial loss (especially in the case of land and more so from rural to urban areas). The market for productive assets, especially land, either for sale or for lease, is highly imperfect. The person possessing assets is therefore likely to leave dependants (family) behind to look after the assets and remit money to them not only for family consumption but for technological development and improvement of the productive assets. Those who possess productive assets but migrate because the assets are not sufficient to provide full employment are more prone to remit for the improvement of the assets and technological developments which would facilitate their return to the areas of origin. Even if we now drop the assumption of one worker in the family (household), the essential conclusions arrived at above remain the same.

Some points emerge sharply from the above analysis. Out-migration from rural to urban areas will be dominated by individual rather than family migration. In such cases, there is greater likelihood of a flow of remittances. So far as the migration of non-asset holders is concerned, there are likely to be remittances at least for the support of the family left behind. If remittances are large enough, these may be used for the purchase of land because traditionally the rural people of India have a great attachment to land. The attachment to land is also a factor which influences some persons who possess land to leave their families behind and to remit money for family consumption, expenditure related to cultivation (including technological development), and improvement and purchase of land.

It is needless to emphasise that in rural areas with strong feudal traditions, the preference will be to use remittances for the purchase of land rather than the improvement of productive assets. But the improvement of productive assets in rural areas depends not only on the inflow of resources and information arising out of migration but also on the public policies which are responsible for the development of infrastructure which is a necessary condition for the improvement of agricultural technology and an increase in production.

In the case of those who do not possess any productive assets, the surplus labour situation in rural areas is sufficient to encourage out-migration of the unemployed and underemployed (Joshi and Joshi, 1976). Theoretically, in this case there is a greater probability that the entire family will out-migrate, possibly after a time-lag. Even those who are employed may out-migrate if the wage rate at the place they intend to migrate to is high enough to compensate for the cost of moving. This is not fully in conformity with Todaro's model in so far as his model suggests that the decision to migrate from rural to urban areas depends on prevailing wage rates and expectations about obtaining employment in the formal sector in urban areas (Todaro, 1969, 1976). Some urban in-migrants may belong to the Todaro type who migrate with a view to getting absorbed in the unorganised sector initially but the modern sector eventually. But a significant proportion of those who migrate from the rural areas in India are used to being unemployed or underemployed and hope to be absorbed in the informal sector and remain in that sector. The underlying causes of migration are, of course, rural-urban income differentials arising out of differentials in earning and/or employment opportunities. The above theoretical formulation implicitly suggests that, *ceteris paribus*, out-migration flows from rural areas will be low where the rate of overall economic growth and infrastructural development is high and balanced and that, in such cases, family migration will be still lower.

It is a well-known fact that the migration process is selective as it does not generally involve all sections of the population equally. Given the basic economic conditions for migration, the social characteristics of migrants depend on the well-known sociological theories of development which emphasise that young males are more likely to migrate. For cultural and social reasons, females in India migrate mainly for marriage, migrating with the husbands or to join the migrant relations. But this may not be the pattern in all developing nations. There is some evidence that in many Latin American and African countries and in some Asian countries like Thailand and the

Philippines the economic reasons for female migration are no less important than family considerations. Young people dominate the migration flows because the return on investment in human capital declines with age. Older people also tend to develop stronger attachments to their property and family. Moreover, migration for both marriage and education are common among younger age groups. The unmarried are also more likely to dominate migration flows, since they do not generally have as much attachment to their families as married people.

With regard to education, the historical process of change has meant that rural India is dominated by activities which do not require much education or skill (except the traditional skills related to primitive agriculture and animal husbandry) whereas many activities in urban areas require some education. The proportion of white-collar jobs is extremely small in rural areas. According to the feudal ethos prevailing in large parts of India, manual work is considered of low status. Moreover, the earnings differential between white-collar jobs or even blue-collar jobs requiring technical education and unskilled and manual work is proportionately higher in urban than in rural areas. Thus rural-urban income differentials are higher for the educated than for the uneducated. The educated are also better informed about job prospects outside their locality. Because of all these factors there is usually a relatively higher propensity among the educated to out-migrate from rural areas.

In the case of migration to acquire education, the choice is not simply between a better education in the city and a less good one in the rural areas, but also between additional education in the city and little or no further education in the rural areas. Rural-urban migration for education is, therefore, not uncommon among young people in India. An interesting aspect in this context is that young people with some education who may be facing unemployment in the rural areas (because of the lack of sufficient jobs for the educated), migrate to urban areas to acquire further education and skills but end up as wage earners. Although migrants from rural areas tend to be better educated than those who stay behind, they often have less education than those already living in the urban areas. Paradoxically, then, rural-urban migration may lower the average level of education both in the rural area of origin and in the urban destination.

This theoretical formulation therefore suggests that rural-urban migration in a surplus labour situation is likely to improve the level of employment and income of out-migrant households. There is also likely to be an improvement in household income distribution in the rural areas, unless out-migration and the associated flow of remittances are relatively more among the rural rich. Further, the inflow of resources and information may result in technological development and increased production, provided public policies have created the infrastructural conditions necessary for development.

In large parts of rural India where the population is enmeshed in feudal tradition, working for others as a labourer or even working manually on one's own land is often considered to be of low status. An upper caste person (for example a Brahmin or a Rajput) is forbidden by social custom to touch a plough. If he owns a small plot of land which he cannot use profitably by hiring labour, he leases it out on a share-cropping basis instead of cultivating it himself. This is one among many reasons for share-cropping cultivation, which is inefficient from the point of view of land productivity and generally hampers technological development in a situation of land scarcity. Similarly a potter or carpenter in a rural area with a feudal ethos would often cling to his profession, using primitive tools, preferring to subsist rather than work as a labourer. Even an upper caste Hindu (say, a Rajput) may hesitate to accept the job of a guard in his own area but be willing to accept such a job in a distant urban area. Migration flows from rural to urban areas thus often weaken these feudal traditions. With resource and information inflow and an improved understanding of the dignity of labour, the share-cropping system may, therefore, gradually give way to self-cultivation. A carpenter moving to an urban furniture factory to work as a labourer, or any self-employed person becoming a wage earner in the town, is likely to acquire new skills and tools and may thus encourage the adoption of new techniques in the rural areas. It is true that the breaking down of the share-cropping system, the changing of attitudes to manual jobs among high-status rural people, and improvements in technology are usually long run phenomena, but their effect on the acceptance of modern values with regard to the dignity of labour and associated work culture is almost inevitable with some time lag.

The macro level effects of migration on the rural areas from where the out-migration takes place largely depend on the magnitude of the migration flow and the quantum of resource inflow in the rural belt. If migration takes place in an economic situation which is poised for rapid and healthy industrialization, not only will the rate of rural-urban migration be high but the inflow of resources to the rural areas will also be large. The rural areas will feel the impact of a reduction in unemployment, disguised unemployment and income inequality and an added impetus to technological development. In the urban areas migration will strengthen the small scale industrialization process, and its secondary impact in terms of the expansion of trade and commerce both in rural and urban areas will dynamize the entire economy. Some evidence of this is available from the Punjab study referred to in Chapter 1. However, since migration is a selective process and out-migration is usually dominated by young, skilled, motivated and achievement-oriented persons, this may lead to a deterioration in the quality of rural labour, if not a shortage of labour in a labour surplus economy. But this does not necessarily imply that all or even the best of the young, skilled, motivated and achievement-oriented out-migrate. Some of them are left behind and may take up the challenge of rural development when they are aided by an inflow of resources and information.

There was a sharp decline in the growth of industrial production in India during the latter half of the sixties (Ahluwalia, 1985), and the economy was plagued with increasing industrial sickness during the 1970s and early 1980s. In 1983, the number of small industrial units reporting sick was more than 78,000 accounting for about 10 per cent of all units registered with the Small Industries Development Organization (SIDO). The number of large industrial units (availing themselves of bank credit of Rs 10 million or more) declared sick had increased from 241 in December 1976 to 513 by June 1984. The data presented in table 2.1 indicate that the three states selected for the present study do not show a high rate of growth of either agricultural or industrial production. Bihar is the poorest state in terms of both growth of production (table 2.1) and per capita income (table 2.2). Both Kerala and Uttar Pradesh, on the other hand, are middle level states in terms of per capita income. However, agricultural growth is negligible in Kerala, though Uttar Pradesh shows a moderate rate of growth both in industrial and in agricultural production. But among the three states, Kerala is relatively more industrialised, with a diversified economy. The percentage of industrial workers to total workers is 16.1 in Kerala, whereas it is 6.3 and 10.4 in Bihar and Uttar Pradesh respectively. The overall low share of industrial workers in total employment suggests a low level of industrialization in all three states. In addition, there is the problem of increasing industrial sickness. This scenario, associated with the rather low rate of growth of agricultural production (with the exception of Uttar Pradesh) would imply moderate out-migration from rural to urban areas, but dominated by distress migration and, therefore, involving a low level of remittances and a still lower use of remittances for productive purposes.

The consequences of in-migration in urban areas are likely to be mixed. Given the prevailing structure of the industrial and trading sectors in the urban areas of the three selected states, in-migrants from rural areas are more likely to crowd the informal sector (Kannapan, 1983). Since the wages and earnings of the self-employed in this sector are usually at subsistence level, the effects are likely to be the replacement of child labour by adult labour and more intensive use of labour (for example, repairs taking the place of replacements), without any adverse effects on wage rates. Marginal efficiency of investment is therefore likely to increase.

Table 2.1: Annual compound rate of growth of industrial and agricultural production (1969–70 to 1983–84)

States	Industrial production			
	Registered units	Unregistered units	All units	Agricultural production
(1)	(2)	(3)	(4)	(5)
Andhra Pradesh	7.23	3.75	5.47	3.31
Bihar	9.16	−7.79	0.45	0.49
Gujarat	3.40	3.42	3.40	3.92
Haryana	8.54	5.69	7.66	3.31
Karnataka	6.65	4.36	5.62	2.44
Kerala	4.91	6.52	5.52	0.23
Madhya Pradesh	9.34	4.95	7.37	1.65
Maharashtra	5.34	3.81	5.02	5.59
Orissa	0.67	2.61	1.38	2.28
Punjab	7.02	6.07	6.57	3.92
Rajasthan	6.89	0.45	3.52	2.47
Tamil Nadu	4.75	3.00	4.05	1.12
Uttar Pradesh	6.01	7.45	6.77	3.19
West Bengal	0.69	2.48	1.16	0.91

Sources: of date in columns 2, 3 and 4: Brochure on Estimates of State Domestic Product, Nov. 1985 and June 1988, Central Statistical Organization, Government of India, New Delhi; and for column 5: Commission of Agricultural Costs and Prices, Government of India, *Report for kharif crops of 1985–86 season* (mimeograph), 1986, p. 69.

Table 2.2: Per capita income at current prices (in rupees)

States (1)	1960–61 (2)	1965–66 (3)	1970–71 (4)	1980–81 (5)	1984–85 (6)	1986–87 (P) (7)
Andhra Pradesh	275	387	585	1 358	2 034	2 333
Bihar	215	332	402	943	1 513	1 802
Gujarat	362	498	829	1 968	3 118	3 515
Haryana	327	450	877	2 351	3 230	3 925
Karnataka	296	448	641	1 454	2 189	2 486
Kerala	259	380	594	1 385	2 104	2 371
Madhya Pradesh	252	298	484	1 181	1 699	2 020
Maharashtra	409	534	783	2 244	3 177	3 743
Orissa	217	329	478	1 173	1 671	2 024
Punjab	366	562	1 070	2 620	4 103	4 954
Rajasthan	284	373	651	1 224	2 045	2 145
Tamil Nadu	334	403	581	1 324	2 173	2 732
Uttar Pradesh	252	373	486	1 272	1 784	2 146
West Bengal	390	532	722	1 643	2 576	2 864
INDIA	306	426	633	1 559	2 344	2 824*

(P) Provisional.

* Estimated by applying the growth rates of new series (1980–81 base) of National Accounts.

Source: Central Statistical Organization, Government of India, *Estimates of State Domestic Product*, 1988.

With regard to urban-urban migration, the logical formulation would suggest that wage earners move from one urban area to another in search of better employment and income opportunities. The self-employed and employers also move because of better trade and business prospects in larger cities. In such cases fixed assets are generally not physically transferred from one urban centre to another. These are usually converted into money capital for transfer purposes because the asset market is more developed in urban than in rural areas. Urban-urban migration is therefore more likely to be dominated by family rather than individual migration and is also likely to be associated with a low level of remittances to the rural areas (Oberai and Singh, 1983).

The negative aspect of urban in-migration is related to overcrowding and congestion in the cities. If the civic authorities are not alive to the extent of migration flows and the conditions under which these flows occur, and do not take appropriate policy measures, the conditions of urban life are likely to deteriorate. There will be unplanned and unauthorized constructions and encroachment on public lands, which may be associated with frequent demolition squads, resistance to these, and concomitant social tension and increased lawlessness, resulting in further growth of the lumpenproletariat.

Thus, while the consequences of migration for the individual migrants and their households are more likely to be positive, the overall consequences for the rural and urban areas cannot be determined on the basis of a logical framework alone. These need to be examined empirically in particular socio-economic situations if meaningful policy implications are to be derived.

CHAPTER 3

FLOWS AND CHARACTERISTICS
OF MIGRANTS

The consequences of migration, as discussed in the previous chapter. largely depend on the type of migrants who dominate the migration flows. Thus without sufficient knowledge of specific migrant characteristics, the formulation of appropriate policies is severely handicapped.

The purpose of this section is to provide an overview of the migration flows in the rural areas of the three selected states and to examine the extent to which the process of migration is selective, particularly with respect to age, sex, education and social background.

3.1 *Rates of migration*

The rural migration flow in all the three selected states is dominated by out-migration (table 3.1). In-migration for reasons other than marriage is almost negligible in Bihar because of its low level of agricultural growth and also because, unlike Kerala, rural Bihar has a low level of economic diversification. That is why Kerala has higher return-migration rates than both Bihar and Uttar Pradesh. Moreover, out-migrants from Kerala who migrate out of India mostly go for a fixed period of employment, after which many of them return to their areas of origin. The rural areas of Almora district of Uttar Pradesh do, however, show a total in-migration rate of 9.2 per cent, out of which in-migration for reasons other than marriage is almost 4.3 per cent. This is because activities connected with forestry and stonework attract people from outside to Almora, a hilly region of Uttar Pradesh.

3.2 *Characteristics of out-migrants*

The data show that out-migration of women for reasons other than marriage is higher in both Kerala and Uttar Pradesh than in Bihar (table 3.2). This is perhaps due to the fact that the Christian population

Table 3.1: Rates of migration in sample village (percentage)

	In-migration			Out-migration			Return-migrants	Total
	Marriage	other reason	Total	Marriage	Other reason	Total		
Bihar	7.6	0.4	8.0	6.7	8.7	15.4	1.1	100 (32 175)
Kerala	6.1	3.5	9.6	6.7	7.4	14.1	2.2	100 (22 548)
Uttar Pradesh*	4.9	4.3	9.2	6.0	8.0	14.0	0.8	100 (30 639)

Note: Figures in parentheses refer to total population in sample villages.

* Figures refer to Almora District only.

constitutes a significant proportion of the Kerala sample and hill people of the Uttar Pradesh sample. The proportion of females working is generally higher among these two groups which may have led to relatively higher out-migration among them. The proportion of Scheduled Castes/Tribes is almost the same among out-migrants and among the general population in both Bihar and Uttar Pradesh (about 39 per cent and 18 per cent respectively). In Kerala, however, the proportion of Scheduled Castes/Tribes among out-migrants is lower than in the general population. Scheduled Castes/Tribes thus have a lower propensity to out-migrate than other caste and religious groups.

Age selectivity is very much in evidence in the out-migration flows from the rural areas, which are dominated by persons aged 15–30 in Uttar Pradesh, 15–40 in Bihar, and 20–40 in Kerala. Kerala also shows the highest proportion of out-migrants in the 30–40 age group. One important reason for the relatively high out-migration in this age group in Kerala is that the out-migration to Gulf countries requires more experienced people. However, the relatively larger spread of out-migrants among different age groups in rural Bihar is an indication of the distressed conditions there. A further indication of these distressed conditions is the fact that married people dominate the out-migration flow in Bihar, i.e. the proportion of married people out-migrating is higher than the proportion of married people in the sample population. Associated with this is the fact that the proportion of household heads or their spouses among out-migrants is highest in Bihar and lowest in Uttar Pradesh which indicates the relative prosperity of the rural areas of Uttar Pradesh. However, as expected, sons and daughters dominate the out-migration flows from the rural areas in all three states.

Analysis of the out-migration flows in terms of educational levels provides additional evidence that the migration process is selective. In Kerala, those with education levels of secondary and above have a relatively greater propensity to migrate than those with less than secondary education. In Bihar and Uttar Pradesh even those with 'some formal education but less than secondary' have a greater propensity to out-migrate than those with no formal education. The reason may be that the distressed situation in rural Bihar and Uttar Pradesh is pushing about 39 and 56 per cent respectively of those who have not yet achieved secondary level education to migrate to urban areas in search of livelihood (table 3.2).

Table 3.2: Percentage distribution of out-migrants and sample population (10 years and older) by demographic and socio-economic characteristics

	Bihar		Kerala		Uttar Pradesh	
	Out-migrants (1 290)	Sample population (9 209)	Out-migrants (1 192)	Sample population (9 829)	Out-migrants (1 196)	Sample population (8 466)
Religion/Caste						
SC/ST	39.4	38.7	4.6	8.1	17.5	18.1
Hindu other than SC/ST	52.4	54.0	51.0	49.9	81.1	80.1
Muslim	7.3	7.1	12.8	12.4	1.2	1.7
Christian	0.1	0.1	31.2	29.5	0.0	0.0
Others	0.8	0.1	0.4	0.1	0.3	0.1
Sex						
Male	91.1	54.4	85.4	50.6	87.2	54.4
Female	8.9	45.6	14.6	49.4	12.8	45.6
Age (Years)						
10–14	6.4	17.0	1.5	12.0	3.9	14.7
15–19	20.4	13.4	9.7	14.0	30.5	16.6
20–24	27.3	12.9	32.6	16.0	41.1	15.8
25–29	21.4	11.4	27.4	12.5	13.8	10.1
30–39	18.8	16.4	23.1	16.7	7.1	12.9
40 +	5.7	28.9	5.7	28.6	3.6	29.9

Education						
No formal education	43.4	64.3	0.8	9.0	8.5	39.2
Less than secondary	38.7	28.5	61.7	71.2	56.5	39.1
Secondary	14.8	6.1	27.8	15.1	21.5	16.6
Graduate and above	3.3	1.2	9.7	4.7	13.5	5.1
Marital status						
Never married	35.2	35.4	57.6	45.5	50.7	36.3
Married	62.7	57.7	42.2	46.3	47.3	54.7
Relation to head						
Head/spouse	24.6	41.6	11.8	35.1	1.5	38.6
Son/daughter	57.2	38.2	67.5	47.6	66.8	38.4
Others	18.3	20.2	20.7	17.3	31.7	23.0

Note: Numbers are given in parentheses.

SC/ST = Scheduled Caste/Scheduled Tribe.

Table 3.3: Percentage of out-migrants who go to urban areas by level of education

	Bihar	Kerala			Uttar Pradesh
		Within India	Outside India	Total	
No formal education	79.7	33.3	22.2	55.5	81.7
Less than secondary	87.3	29.4	43.1	72.5	82.6
Secondary	76.4	52.3	20.1	72.4	87.2
Graduate and above	82.5	60.1	12.3	72.3	89.0
All	81.6	38.8	33.6	72.4	85.7

With regard to the destination of out-migrants, table 3.3 gives data on the percentage of out-migrants who go to urban areas. The classical pattern of selectivity with respect to destination and educational level is empirically evident in the case of Uttar Pradesh, where there is both a moderate growth of agriculture in the rural areas and of industry in the urban areas. Therefore, not only is the percentage of out-migrants going to urban areas the highest but this percentage increases as a function of educational level. In Kerala, where the rural economy is relatively more diversified (i.e. not as heavily dependent on agriculture as in Bihar and Uttar Pradesh) and there is considerable demand (mainly from Gulf countries) for semi-skilled labour (not essentially educated), the pattern is not much different from that in Uttar Pradesh. The high income differential between areas within and outside India and the specific nature of international demand for semi-skilled labour are responsible for the relatively higher proportion of out-migrants with less than secondary education moving outside India rather than to urban areas within India. In contrast the choice of destination of out-migrants in Bihar is not particularly related to their educational background. This is perhaps because of its poor agriculture, non-diversified rural economy, low level of industrialization and low rate of industrial growth.

The data on the usual activity status of rural out-migrants provide empirical support to the theoretical formulation which suggests that employment and income differentials between origin and destination areas are the primary causes of rural out-migration. In all three states the unemployed have a relatively higher propensity to out-migrate, that is, the proportion of unemployed among the out-migrants is higher than among the sample population (table 3.4). Considering

Table 3.4: Percentage distribution of out-migrants and sample population (10 years and above) by usual activity status

	Bihar		Kerala		Uttar Pradesh	
	Out-migrants (1 290)	Sample population (9 209)	Out-migrants (1 192)	Sample population (9 829)	Out-migrants (1 196)	Sample population (8 466)
Employed	54.7	44.5	35.0	27.5	23.4	35.0
Unemployed	26.8	4.8	51.2	18.2	28.0	6.1
Housekeeping	5.4	23.8	5.7	24.0	12.9	22.5
Student	12.5	15.1	7.7	21.5	33.6	23.4
Others	0.6	10.8	0.5	8.9	2.3	13.0

Note: Numbers are given in parentheses.

unemployed out-migrants as a proportion of total unemployed in the sample population, the figures come out at 78 per cent for Bihar, 65 per cent for Uttar Pradesh and 34 per cent for Kerala. It seems, therefore, that the unemployed are most impoverished in Bihar because even when they do not face as bright a prospect by out-migrating, they show a relatively higher propensity to out-migrate. In Kerala, the fact that a relatively lower propensity to migrate among unemployed is observed may suggest that they are more aware of the difficult labour market conditions elsewhere because of their relatively higher levels of education.

The employed also have a relatively high propensity to out-migrate from rural areas, particularly in Bihar and Kerala. Disguised unemployment and perceived rural-urban income differentials are perhaps the main causes of out-migration among the employed. In Bihar, there is a high level of disguised unemployment. The average number of days employed in a year calculated from the survey data is 213 in Bihar as compared with 292 and 300 in Kerala and Uttar Pradesh respectively. Rural-urban income differentials are also especially pronounced in Bihar because of its poor agriculture. While the index of agricultural production increased annually by about half per cent during the period 1967–84, the population grew by more than two per cent per annum during the same period. In Kerala, the propensity to out-migrate is high among the employed because of migration to other countries.

It will be seen from table 3.5 that while wage/salary earners dominate the out-migration flows in Bihar and Kerala, in Uttar Pradesh the flow is dominated by the self-employed, including unpaid family workers. These unpaid family workers probably come from those farming households who have some agricultural surplus at their disposal (consequent on the Green Revolution) and out-migrate with a view to possible investment and business prospects.

It will also be evident that among the employed in Bihar and Kerala, those who are not in the agricultural sector generally show a slightly greater tendency to out-migrate. In Uttar Pradesh, however, those working in agriculture (either self-employed or wage earners) have a relatively higher propensity to out-migrate. Of the total number of persons employed in the agricultural sector, out-migrants account for 16.6 per cent in Bihar, 11.1 per cent in Kerala and 9.9 per cent in Uttar Pradesh. The corresponding percentages for the non-agricultural sector are 19.6, 21.4 and 8.4 respectively. It is also interesting

Table 3.5: Percentage distribution of employed out-migrants and sample population (10 years and above) by employment status and occupation

Employment status/occupation before migration	Bihar		Kerala		Uttar Pradesh	
	Out-migrants (706)	Sample population (4 134)	Out-migrants (417)	Sample population (2 532)	Out-migrants (280)	Sample population (2 963)
Employment status						
Self-employed	33.3	45.2	12.6	19.1	31.6	40.0
Wage/salary earners	66.7	54.5	86.7	78.7	29.6	35.3
Unpaid family workers	0.0	0.2	0.7	2.2	38.7	24.6
Others	0.0	0.0	0.0	0.0	0.1	0.1
Occupation						
Professional and technical workers	1.5	2.6	6.1	5.7	0.7	0.8
Administration workers	0.3	0.4	1.7	2.6	0.7	0.2
Clerical workers	1.1	0.5	11.1	7.0	5.0	4.7
Trade and sales workers	0.9	2.7	5.4	5.7	6.7	6.2
Service workers	1.9	1.7	4.2	4.8	2.3	5.7
Agricultural sector workers	82.4	84.7	32.2	47.7	72.5	69.2
Production and related workers	11.8	7.4	13.5	6.8	4.3	4.0
Others	0.0	0.0	25.8	19.7	7.7	9.1

Note: Numbers are given in parentheses.

to observe that both clerical workers and production and related workers show a relatively high tendency to out-migrate in all three states, although only marginally in Uttar Pradesh. This is because both these occupations usually account for a significant proportion of urban employment; those employed in these activities in rural areas acquire skill and training in the process and are thus more suitable for jobs in urban areas.

It will be seen that the poor have a relatively higher propensity to out-migrate from the rural areas. In all three states, the bottom three deciles (i.e. the bottom 30 per cent) account for a higher percentage among out-migrants than among the sample population (table 3.6).

While the poorest show a greater propensity to out-migrate from the rural areas, they do not necessarily belong to the landless group. It is in fact the landed who have the greater tendency to out-migrate, except in Bihar (table 3.7). In Bihar the landless appear to be more prone to out-migrate. In Kerala the middle peasantry dominate the out-migration flow. In Uttar Pradesh, on the other hand, all the landed groups except the highest size class of cultivators have a relatively high propensity to out-migrate. This is perhaps indicative of the phenomenon of using agricultural surplus to develop the secondary sector and seems to be associated with the classical pattern of development. This inference is further strengthened when we analyse the landholding status and occupation at the time of out-migration and the destination and present occupation of out-migrants in Uttar Pradesh. The detailed data, although not presented clearly here, show that among out-migrants to urban areas, there are more than three times the number of cultivators than of agricultural labourers.

The empirical facts analysed above suggest not only that out-migration from rural areas is selective but that it is mainly caused by employment and income differentials. These differentials are mainly due to the process of industrialization and unevenness in agricultural development, as noted earlier. There is also some evidence of agricultural surplus moving into urban areas, particularly in Uttar Pradesh, for investment in secondary and tertiary activities. It is in this context that the subjective perceptions of the out-migrants as to their reasons for out-migration become more important.

Table 3.8 provides information about the reasons for out-migration. It is interesting to note that a very large proportion of out-migrants, in all three states, leave the rural areas to look for either employment

Table 3.6: Percentage distribution of out-migrants and sample population (10 years and above) by household income (excluding remittances)

Income class (deciles)	Bihar		Kerala		Uttar Pradesh	
	Out-migrants (1 290)	Sample population (9 209)	Out-migrants (1 192)	Sample population (9 829)	Out-migrants (1 196)	Sample population (8 466)
1	15.8	6.5	17.2	7.9	13.2	7.7
2	12.9	7.5	14.0	6.5	10.7	8.0
3	11.8	8.7	9.0	8.8	7.6	7.4
4	8.2	9.2	6.8	9.0	10.8	10.1
5	8.5	9.0	6.8	9.2	9.2	9.5
6	8.0	10.0	8.2	10.7	9.6	10.9
7	7.9	11.3	8.7	10.8	8.1	10.1
8	8.1	11.7	8.6	10.8	10.7	11.3
9	10.0	12.6	8.8	11.9	8.7	11.8
10	8.9	13.5	11.9	14.4	11.4	13.1

Note: Numbers are given in parentheses.

Table 3.7: Percentage distribution of out-migrants and sample population by landholding status

Landholding status	Bihar		Kerala		Uttar Pradesh	
	Out-migrants (1 290)	Sample population (9 209)	Out-migrants (1 192)	Sample population (9 829)	Out-migrants (1 196)	Sample population (8 466)
Landless	39.0	36.1	8.4	9.7	32.6	34.1
Up to 2.5 acres	38.3	39.6	85.0	85.8	48.7	47.6
2.6–5 acres	13.5	13.8	5.0	3.4	9.9	9.1
5.1–10 acres	6.0	6.9	1.6	0.9	7.7	7.4
10 + acres	3.2	3.6	0.0	0.2	1.1	1.8

Note: Numbers are given in parentheses.

Table 3.8: Percentage distribution of out-migrants by reasons for out-migration

Reasons for out-migration	Bihar	Kerala	Uttar Pradesh
(N)	(1 290)	(1 192)	(1 196)
Search for employment/ better employment	90.8	81.0	72.2
Education	2.6	1.0	8.5
Follow/accompany family	6.3	9.2	13.3
Others*	0.3	8.8	6.0

* Includes job transfer, difficulties in the family, etc.

or better employment. The proportion of such out-migrants is highest (91 per cent) in Bihar, the poorest among the three states, and lowest (72 per cent) in Uttar Pradesh where agriculture is relatively more developed. Education also appears to be an important reason for out-migration in Uttar Pradesh, but not in Bihar and Kerala. In Kerala, the low level of out-migration to acquire education is understandable in view of the relatively better educational infrastructure even in the rural areas.

The out-migrants appear to benefit in terms of both employment and earnings. Among those whose usual activity status before migration was 'unemployed', 96.0, 94.9 and 97.5 per cent became employed after migration in Bihar, Kerala and Uttar Pradesh respectively (table 3.9). In the case of those who were students before migration, more than two-thirds in Bihar and more than three-quarters in Kerala and Uttar Pradesh became part of the labour force after migration. It is also interesting to note that even among those whose usual activity before migration was housekeeping, no less than 14 per cent in Bihar and 25 per cent in Kerala joined the labour force after migration.

There is evidence of a sharp shift in employment and occupational status after migration. The data on employment status before migration given in table 3.5 show that in Uttar Pradesh the self-employed account for about 32 per cent of employed out-migrants. But most of them did not remain in self-employment after migration. In fact, 77.5 per cent became wage/salary earners (table 3.10). In Kerala, the self-employed constitute a smaller proportion (13 per cent) of the out-migrants who were employed before migration, but there too 77.3 per cent became wage/salary earners after migration.

Table 3.9: Percentage distribution of out-migrants by activity status before and after migration

State/activity status before migration	Current activity status					
	Employed	*Un-employed*	*House-keeping*	*Student*	*Others*	*All*
Bihar						
(N = 1 290)						
Employed	96.9	1.6	0.4	0.3	0.7	100.0
Unemployed	96.0	2.5	0.3	0.0	1.2	100.0
Housekeeping	13.6	1.5	84.8	0.0	0.0	100.0
Student	66.9	1.3	0.0	29.0	2.6	100.0
Kerala						
(N = 1 192)						
Employed	96.3	2.5	0.0	0.0	1.2	100.0
Unemployed	94.9	3.0	0.8	0.5	6.8	100.0
Housekeeping	25.4	0.0	73.0	0.0	1.6	100.0
Student	78.4	6.8	0.0	11.4	3.4	100.0
Uttar Pradesh						
(N = 1 196)						
Employed	93.7	1.1	3.3	0.0	1.9	100.0
Unemployed	97.5	2.2	0.0	0.0	0.3	100.0
Housekeeping	4.1	0.0	95.9	0.0	0.0	100.0
Student	73.2	2.8	0.5	22.8	0.8	100.0

In Bihar, the self-employed account for 33 per cent of employed out-migrants, and 82.4 per cent of them became wage-earners.

Among those who were unemployed before migration but took up a job after migration, more than 90 per cent entered into wage employment. The tendency to shift to wage employment is also prominent among unpaid family workers, who account for a substantial number of workers only in Uttar Pradesh.

The analysis of data related to occupational shift, although not presented in the table, indicates that in Uttar Pradesh, though the bulk of the out-migrants who were employed before migration belonged to occupations related to the agricultural sector (72.5 per cent), only 4.6 per cent remained in that sector after migration. In Bihar, 82 per cent of the employed out-migrants were in the agricultural sector before migration, but only 9 per cent of them continued in that sector after their move. This is partly because the level of out-migration to other rural areas is rather low because agriculture remains the most

Table 3.10: Percentage distribution of out-migrants by employment status before and after migration

State/employment and activity status before migration	Employment status after migration		
	Self-employed	Wage/salary earner	All
Bihar			
Employed			
Self-employed	17.6	82.4	100.0
Wage/salary earner	3.2	96.8	100.0
Unemployed	9.6	90.4	100.0
Kerala			
Employed			
Self-employed	22.7	77.3	100.0
Wage/salary earner	1.8	98.2	100.0
Unemployed	2.4	97.6	100.0
Uttar Pradesh			
Employed			
Self-employed	22.4	77.5	100.0
Wage/salary earner	1.2	98.8	100.0
Unemployed	6.1	93.9	100.0

underdeveloped in Bihar among the three states. The shift from agriculture is not so pronounced in Kerala, partly because the proportion of out-migrants employed in the agricultural sector before migration is relatively lower in Kerala than in Uttar Pradesh and Bihar. In Kerala, the agricultural sector accounts for only 32 per cent of the employed out-migrants and about 54 per cent of them continued in that occupation after migration.

In production related occupations, the shift is not so pronounced. In Uttar Pradesh nearly half of those employed in such occupations before migration remained in them, while both in Kerala and in Bihar nearly 78 per cent continued to do so. In addition, many of the out-migrants who were unemployed before migration or were not in the labour force at all, such as those engaged in housekeeping, etc., also joined the ranks of the employed (the rate of employment among the out-migrants increased by 158 per cent in Bihar, 258 per cent in Kerala and 327 per cent in Uttar Pradesh), and a sizeable number of these went for production related occupations. The net effect is that production related occupations account for 63, 15 and 23 per cent of employed migrants in Bihar, Kerala and Uttar Pradesh respectively.

The data also show that clerical work is an important occupation among out-migrants after migration, accounting for 7, 16 and 23 per cent respectively in Bihar, Kerala and Uttar Pradesh. Similar in importance is the service sector, accounting for 11, 12 and 20 per cent of employed out-migrants respectively. Trade and sales work, which is an important occupation in urban areas, does not seem to attract many migrants. It accounts for only 6.7, 5.5 and 7.6 per cent of employed out-migrants respectively.

The distribution of out-migrants by monthly income (table 3.11) reveals that the modal monthly income in all three states lies in the range of Rs 500–1,000. The average monthly income is Rs 715, Rs 1,346 and Rs 655 in Bihar, Kerala and Uttar Pradesh respectively. The relatively higher average income for out-migrants in Kerala (and the fact that for no less than 23.3 per cent of out-migrants the monthly income range is as high as Rs 2,000–4,000) is due to the relatively higher earnings of out-migrants who go to other countries.

Table 3.11: Percentage distribution of out-migrants by current monthly income

Monthly income	Bihar	Kerala	Uttar Pradesh
None	17.0	11.9	24.0
Less than Rs 250	10.1	2.6	2.4
Rs 250–500	29.0	11.4	17.7
Rs 500–1,000	36.4	33.4	46.8
Rs 1,000–2,000	3.8	14.5	7.7
Rs 2,000–4,000	0.9	23.3	0.6
Rs 4,000 and above	2.8	2.7	0.8
Mean income (Rs)	715	1 346	655

3.3   *Characteristics of return-migrants*

The migration flow is not always uni-directional. It is a well-known phenomenon that some out-migrants return to their place of origin. They may come back if they fail to achieve the objectives with which they out-migrated or because they cannot reconcile themselves to the social environment and way of life in the destination areas. They may also return if they went for a fixed contract period or after completing their service tenure. Some successful out-migrants may also find it more worthwhile to return to their native home and make use there of the skill/wealth acquired during their stay away.

An interesting aspect of return migration is that the infl... experience, information and resources is likely to improv... socio-economic position of the place of origin, provided the demonstration effect related to consumerism is not powerful enough to affect the investment process adversely. Although, as noted earlier, the rate of return migration is not very high, especially in Bihar and Uttar Pradesh, it is interesting to note the places from where migrants are returning. Table 3.12 suggests that, in Bihar, the percentage of out-migrants returning from the urban areas is not only high but it is actually higher than the percentage of out-migrants to urban areas from rural Bihar (see table 3.3). In Kerala and Uttar Pradesh, however, the situation is exactly the opposite.

Table 3.12: Percentage distribution of return migrants by previous place of residence

Previous place of residence	Bihar	Kerala	Uttar Pradesh
Rural areas	13.1	36.1	22.9
Urban areas	86.9	63.9	77.1
Total	100.0	100.0	100.0
Within district	13.7	14.2	37.9
Outside district but within state	16.7	36.8	27.9
Outside state but within India	69.5	23.3	34.2
Outside India	0.0	25.5	0.0
Total	100.0	100.0	100.0

In Kerala 19.1 per cent of return migrants came back because they had saved enough money to set up a business in their area of origin (table 3.13). Of these, 34.2 per cent returned from outside India, 23.6 per cent from rural areas within India and 42.2 per cent from urban areas within India. Unlike in Kerala, investment in business is not an important factor in return-migration in Uttar Pradesh. On the other hand, retirement (after attaining old age) is an important reason in Uttar Pradesh but not in Kerala. In Uttar Pradesh, 34.1 per cent returned after retirement; of these, 15.3 per cent returned from rural areas and 84.7 per cent from urban areas. The end of employment because of completion of a contract is a major factor in Kerala, accounting for 47.7 per cent of return migration. Among these, 48 per cent returned from outside India and 52 per cent from within India. This reason accounts for only 3.2 per cent of return migration in Uttar Pradesh. Job transfer, which sometimes brings government employees back to their origin area, is responsible for 27.7 per cent of return migration in Kerala. Failure to become reconciled with the life-style of the place of destination and absence of job satisfaction (maybe because of the low level of income) account for 15.7 and 5.5 per cent of return-migration in Uttar Pradesh and Kerala respectively. This is also an important reason in Bihar, accounting for 19.4 per cent of return-migrants. In Bihar another 7.1 per cent of the return-migrants attributed their return to illness. The most important reasons for return, however, are retirement and completion of work, which together accounted for 33 per cent of the return-migrants. Another, almost equally important, reason is industrial unrest (continual strikes, etc.), which forced 23.2 per cent of the return-migrants to come back.

Table 3.13: Percentage distribution of return-migrants by reasons for return

Reasons for returning	Bihar	Kerala	Uttar Pradesh
Job terminated	21.6	47.7	3.2
Retirement	11.4	0.0	34.1
Job transfer	1.4	27.7	4.9
Strike, etc.	23.2	0.0	0.0
Did not like place/job	19.4	5.5	15.7
Illness	7.1	0.0	4.3
To set up business in place of origin	0.0	19.1	0.0
Needed back in family	11.8	0.0	23.7
Followed family	3.8	0.0	3.8
Others	0.0	0.0	6.4
All	100.0	100.0	100.0
(N)	(211)	(220)	(185)

Among the return-migrants, 47.6 per cent in Bihar, 62.8 per cent in Kerala and 55.8 per cent in Uttar Pradesh had sent money while they were away and also brought money back with them. The percentage who neither brought money nor ever sent money was 18 per cent in Bihar and Kerala and 22 per cent in Uttar Pradesh. This shows that a significant proportion of return-migrants who are employed while away are able to send or bring back some resources to their place of origin.

The data presented in table 3.14 show that a relatively large propor-

Table 3.14: Some characteristics of return-migrants (percentage)

	Bihar	Kerala	Uttar Pradesh
Married	70.1	39.7	54.8
Employed at the time of out-migration	70.8	32.3	48.9
With no formal education	62.3	.2.2	21.3
Returned within a year	27.7	12.2	10.2
Acquired skill while away	4.7	14.0	21.0
Sent and/or brought money	81.9	81.5	78.0
Average amount brought at the time of return (Rs)	(1 385)	(5 637)	(6 562)

tion of return-migrants in Bihar are married as compared with the other two states. The percentage of those who return within a year is also highest in Bihar, that is 27.7. The corresponding percentages for Kerala and Uttar Pradesh are 12.2 and 10.2 respectively. Bihar thus presents a case where internal migration is taking place in an economic situation where both the level of economic development and the rate of economic growth are low. There is some evidence of distress out-migration associated with return-migration which includes some failures. This is why there tends to be a low inflow of resources and not much acquisition of skills by the return-migrants. Since one important factor dominating the out-migration flow in Kerala is a large income differential for the semi-skilled jobs requiring moderate education for those out-migrating to Gulf countries, the benefits of resource inflow as opposed to skill acquisition are more pronounced in Kerala than in Uttar Pradesh. Although there is hardly any evidence of brain drain in the context of out-migration flows in the sample as a whole, out-migration nevertheless remains associated with skill acquisition and resource inflow.

CHAPTER 4

REMITTANCES FROM OUT-MIGRANTS AND THEIR EFFECT ON THE LEVEL AND DISTRIBUTION OF RURAL HOUSEHOLD INCOME

The remittances sent by rural out-migrants are an important aspect of the migration process. In the theoretical formulation, presented in section 2, it was noted that remittances from out-migrants may be used either for consumption or for the efficient use and improvement of productive assets. Amongst the poorer sections of society, however, a larger proportion of remittances is likely to be spent on consumption rather than on investment. Yet another hypothesis that emerges from such a framework relates to the role of remittances vis-à-vis rural income inequality. To the extent that remittances are more prevalent in the poorer households, this would normally result in a reduction in rural income inequalities, unless the size of remittances to richer households is large enough to offset the effect of the relatively lower proportion of remitters among these households.

In order to determine which type of out-migrants are more likely to send remittances, table 4.1 presents the socio-economic and demographic characteristics of out-migrants who have ever remitted. The data show considerable regional differences in the proportion of remitters. This proportion is the highest in Bihar (the most under-developed region among the three states), followed by Kerala and then Uttar Pradesh. It is probably the poverty in Bihar which compels even the 'other relations' of the head of the family to remit, and the percentage of remitters for such out-migrants is as high as 76, whereas in Kerala and Uttar Pradesh these percentages are only 43.7 and 33.5 respectively. In Uttar Pradesh (because of its relatively high level of agricultural development), the unmarried do not feel the same compulsion to remit as married out-migrants, who have to support the family at home. The proportion of remitters is, therefore, lower among unmarried than among married people in Uttar Pradesh, but this difference does not exist in Bihar and Kerala. In each of the three regions, the proportion of out-migrants who have ever remitted is lower among those with no formal education than among those with some formal education. This is probably explained by the fact that the incomes of such out-migrants are likely to be too low to allow remittances.

With respect to present place of residence, the proportion of remitters among those who out-migrate to urban areas outside the state is higher than among other categories of out-migrants. Indeed, it is interesting to note that among out-migrants who go to urban areas within India, the proportion of remitters increases with distance. But no such clear pattern can be observed among out-migrants to rural areas. Kerala is the only region in the sample which shows considerable out-migration abroad, the sample for Uttar Pradesh being too small. The proportion of remitters is highest in this category (89.7 per cent), mainly because this category is dominated by out-migration for a limited period, family out-migration is usually not permitted, and income differentials are very high.

In both Uttar Pradesh and Bihar, the proportion of remitters increases as a function of years since migration. This is because the out-migrants take some time to settle; they then gradually acquire skill and experience which finally enable them to increase their income, thus making remittances more possible. This usual pattern is not apparent in Kerala, probably because of the substantial number of Gulf migrants, for most of whom jobs are arranged before migration and the question of a settling down period is therefore not relevant. In the case of Bihar and Uttar Pradesh, the fairly long settling period revealed by the data may, however, indicate the hard living conditions in the urban centres of these two states. The data further show that the proportion of remitters does not decline over time in any of the three states. There is thus no evidence that out-migrants loosen their ties with the origin households as the duration of their stay in the city increases. The fact that the proportion of remitters does not decline over time may also indicate the continuing dependence of the poor origin households on remittances.

While, in Uttar Pradesh, the proportion of remitters is generally lower among the landless than among the landed, in both Kerala and Bihar the pattern is reversed. Moreover, the proportion of remitters

Table 4.1: Percentage of out-migrants who have ever sent remittances by demographic and socio-economic characteristics

Characteristics	Bihar		Kerala		Uttar Pradesh	
	(N)	*% remitted*	*(N)*	*% remitted*	*(N)*	*% remitted*
All	1 026	71.5	1 184	67.1	1 144	46.7
Relationship to head						
Head/spouse	82	65.9	132	97.7	18	33.3
Son/daughter	548	69.2	798	69.5	747	53.7
Others	396	76.0	254	43.7	379	33.5
Marital status						
Never married	223	78.9	439	67.2	398	36.7
Married	776	78.4	739	67.3	719	53.4
Education						
No formal education	417	65.5	8	25.0	115	23.5
Less than secondary	416	76.4	731	70.7	645	48.1
Secondary	157	74.5	326	62.9	193	59.6
Graduate and above	27	70.4	119	59.7	192	43.2
Present place of residence						
Within district						
Rural	125	72.0	135	31.1	88	47.7
Urban	140	62.1	182	48.4	328	37.2
Outside district (within state)						
Rural-	15	66.7	90	66.7	38	26.3
Urban	81	66.7	141	64.5	303	49.8
Outside state						
Rural	44	63.6	51	60.8	35	51.4
Urban	581	76.1	188	67.6	323	56.0
Abroad	—	—	397	89.7	3	33.3
Years since out-migration						
Less than 1	81	46.9	88	59.1	334	42.2
1 to less than 3	203	60.6	297	68.4	283	41.3
3 to less than 5	220	64.1	245	68.2	212	49.5
5 to less than 10	176	79.5	368	67.4	289	54.7
10 +	336	85.4	185	67.0	21	61.9
Land status of household						
Landless	455	73.0	97	76.3	389	35.2
Up to 1 acre	232	64.7	854	70.8	367	69.2
1.1–2.5 acres	215	68.4	156	60.9	205	50.7
2.6–5.0 acres	146	60.3	66	33.3	119	37.8
5.1–7.5 acres	37	78.4	11	27.3	57	21.1
7.6–10.0 acres	26	53.8	5	0.0	33	6.1
10 + acres	31	56.7	—	—	13	15.4

Table 4.1 (*Contd.*)

Characteristics	Bihar		Kerala		Uttar Pradesh	
	(N)	*% remitted*	*(N)*	*% remitted*	*(N)*	*% remitted*
Household income decile						
1	194	76.3	209	87.1	164	66.5
2	157	70.1	169	74.0	125	64.0
3	135	65.2	103	72.8	91	57.1
4	90	62.2	79	75.9	135	42.2
5	92	68.5	88	60.2	112	50.0
6	88	71.6	97	69.1	110	43.6
7	92	65.2	102	49.0	98	44.9
8	95	67.4	100	58.0	124	36.3
9	107	67.3	100	65.0	102	30.4
10	92	58.7	143	44.8	131	28.2
Percentage of household members working						
None	301	80.4	442	78.1	166	51.8
Less than 25	387	72.9	465	63.4	381	41.2
26–50	293	58.4	247	58.3	509	46.2
51–75	99	55.6	35	40.0	92	58.7
More than 75	62	45.2	2	0.0	46	60.9

among the landed decreases as a function of land-size group in both Kerala and Uttar Pradesh, while there is no such clear trend in Bihar. This finding, along with the fact that the overall proportion of remitters is lowest in Uttar Pradesh and highest in Bihar, may suggest that the need of out-migrant families for remittances is much higher in agriculturally poor regions like Bihar and Kerala. This conclusion is further reinforced when we examine the proportion of remitters among out-migrants from various income decile groups. In each of the three states, the proportions of remitters show a generally decreasing trend as we move from lower to higher income deciles, although the trend is weak in Bihar. This shows that in the case of Bihar, even the relatively rich households depend on remittances, which may be because of the higher level of absolute poverty in the state.

As regards the percentage of household members working (which indicates the degree of dependency of the parent household on the out-migrant), we again notice two different trends. In Bihar and Kerala, a lower percentage of workers back home does indicate a higher degree of dependency and is consequently associated with a higher proportion of remitters. But in Uttar Pradesh (where agriculture is more developed), a lower percentage of workers does not necessarily mean greater dependence on the out-migrant and, as such, the proportion of remitters does not necessarily increase.

Table 4.2 presents information about the regularity of remittances for those who have ever remitted. In Bihar and Kerala, the bulk of those who had ever remitted money had sent their latest remittances within two months of the survey. In fact, more than 90 per cent had remitted within the prior six months, indicating a high degree of regularity. This pattern is uniform for all out-migrants regardless of number of years since out-migration. Uttar Pradesh, on the other hand, presents a different picture. There the highest percentage (53.8) of ever remitters had sent their most recent remittances more than a year before the survey and this proportion is even higher

Table 4.2: Percentage distribution of out-migrants who have ever sent remittances by period since last remittance was sent and years since migration

Period since last remittance was sent	Years since migration			
	0–4	5–9	10+	All
Bihar				
0–2 months	79.6	87.4	78.8	80.8
3–5 months	12.3	7.9	14.9	12.4
6–12 months	3.7	3.1	4.3	3.8
More than 1 year	4.5	1.6	2.0	2.9
All	100.0	100.0	100.0	100.0
(N)	(269)	(127)	(255)	(651)
Kerala				
0–2 months	74.4	68.5	69.8	71.7
3–5 months	20.4	20.7	19.4	20.3
6–12 months	3.7	6.8	3.1	4.6
More than 1 year	1.5	4.0	7.8	3.3
All	100.0	100.0	100.0	100.0
(N)	(402)	(251)	(129)	(782)
Uttar Pradesh				
0–2 months	5.9	1.3	0.0	4.4
3–5 months	27.8	1.9	15.4	19.7
6–12 months	29.4	6.9	7.7	22.2
More than 1 year	36.8	89.9	76.9	53.8
All	100.0	100.0	100.0	100.0
(N)	(356)	(159)	(13)	(528)

among out-migrants of longer duration. This slow down in the frequency of remittances from out-migrants of longer duration in Uttar Pradesh and the absence of the same phenomenon elsewhere again suggest how much stronger is the need for remittances in backward areas than in relatively prosperous areas. It should be noted, however, that in Uttar Pradesh, although the frequency of remittances declines over time, no such decline is noticeable in the proportion of remitters.

As far as size of remittances is concerned, the data collected from the surveys are limited to only one year, 1983–84. The mean value of remittances given in table 4.3 shows that out-migrants from cultivating households remit more than those from non-cultivating households in all three states. However, the difference is more pronounced in Kerala. The difference in the size of remittances received by cultivating and non-cultivating households generally persists even when considered with respect to the destination of out-migrants (rural or urban) and years since out-migration, except in some cases in Uttar Pradesh. The fact that out-migrants from cultivating households remit more than those from non-cultivating households may be for two reasons. First, they may be remitting more for the upkeep and improvement of land and other agricultural assets. Second, their earning capacity may be relatively higher and they are, therefore, able to remit more. This is particularly likely to be the case since they tend to have a superior educational background and a relatively larger proportion go to urban areas. The data in fact show that those who go to urban areas remit more than those who migrate to rural areas. The positive correlation of size of remittances with earnings of out-migrants is also supported by the fact that among cultivating households in each of the three states, the mean value of remittances from wage/salary earners is higher than that from the self-employed. Here the implicit assumption, which holds true in the light of our data from the urban survey, is that the self-employed out-migrant earns, on average, less than the wage/salary earner (see Chapter 9). In the case of non-cultivating households, however, self-employed out-migrants send, on average, larger remittances than wage/salary earners. This may be largely because rural artisans who out-migrate from the rural areas can earn relatively higher incomes and are thus able to remit more. The need and attachment of those relations who are left behind are also important considerations influencing the quantum of remittances. This is reflected in the higher mean value of remittances from married out-migrants than from the 'never-

Table 4.3: **Mean remittances per remitting out-migrant during 1983–84 by present place of residence, years since migration, employment status, marital status, education and type of origin household (in rupees)**

	Bihar		Kerala		Uttar Pradesh	
	Cultivating households (N = 466)	Non-cultivating households (N = 325)	Cultivating households (N = 725)	Non-cultivating households (N = 75)	Cultivating households (N = 423)	Non-cultivating households (N = 137)
All	2 421	2 210	5 108	3 824	2 401	2 359
Present place of residence						
Rural (within India)	2 100	1 982	2 104	2 036	2 254	2 057
Urban (within India)	2 429	2 247	2 373	2 145	2 358	2 371
Abroad	—	—	8 392	8 068	9 600*	—
Years since out-migration						
Less than 1	1 141	1 271	2 190	825*	2 124	1 879
1 to less than 3	1 821	1 665	4 873	4 122	2 153	2 250
3 to less than 5	2 197	2 195	5 132	4 444	2 490	2 357
5 to less than 10	2 659	2 502	5 507	4 886	2 247	2 457
10+	2 696	2 517	5 798	2 575*	2 749	2 650
Current employment status						
Self-employed	2 054	2 413	1 601	—	2 139	3 194
Wage/salary earner	2 471	2 212	5 214	3 873	2 413	2 240
Marital status						
Never married	1 668	1 688	4 172	3 418	2 029	2 034
Married	2 553	2 307	5 664	4 274	2 444	2 504
Education						
No formal education	2 022	1 870	6 000	200*	2 066	2 487
Less than secondary	2 321	2 390	5 457	4 186*	2 369	1 936
Secondary	2 706	3 576	4 237	2 944	2 410	2 270
Graduate and above	933*	3 561	5 330	3 020	2 333	3 113

* Figure based on less than 10 observations.

married'. It is, however, interesting to note that in Bihar the size of remittances increases with the level of education of the out-migrants, while the relationship is noticeably different in Uttar Pradesh and Kerala. In Uttar Pradesh, educated out-migrants do not appear to send more than the relatively less educated, possibly because they come from richer households and hence are not under any compulsion to send more. In the case of Kerala, many of the out-migrants to Gulf countries are relatively less educated, but they are able to remit more because of their higher incomes.

The remittances received are put to different uses. It is evident from table 4.4 that more than 70 per cent of both cultivating and non-cultivating households spend the remittances on such basic needs as food and clothing or household goods. This percentage is highest in Bihar and lowest in Uttar Pradesh. Expenditure on education is another important item in Uttar Pradesh and to some extent in Bihar. In Uttar Pradesh, again, about 10 per cent of the receiving households invest in land for residential purposes or in construction and improvement of residential buildings. Further, about 9 per cent of cultivating households have used remittances for investment in farming or business. These are not significant items of expenditure in Bihar or Kerala. This shows that in relatively agriculturally prosperous Uttar Pradesh, at least some households are channelling their resources towards investment both in real estate and in farming or business. It is also interesting to note that in Uttar Pradesh, a relatively larger proportion of cultivating households are using their remittances for education (i.e. building up of human capital) and investment in productive assets as compared with non-cultivating households. This may be largely because the non-cultivating households do not have adequate opportunities to invest in productive assets in rural areas. In fact the data presented in table 4.4 show that a relatively larger proportion of non-cultivating households are using remittances for the purchase or improvement of residential buildings, and a very small proportion (1.1 per cent) for investment in business.

Table 4.5 shows that in all three states the percentage of out-migrant households receiving remittances is high in the lower income deciles. It also shows that remittances constitute a large proportion of income in the lower income deciles in each state. In Bihar and Kerala, two-thirds or more of the total income of out-migrant households in the three lowest income deciles comes from remittances. Remittances are thus the major source of income for poorer households in these

Table 4.4: Percentage distribution of households that have received remittances during 1983–84 by major items on which remittances were spent

	Bihar		Kerala		Uttar Pradesh	
	Cultivating households	Non-cultivating households	Cultivating households	Non-cultivating households	Cultivating households	Non-cultivating households
Purchase of land for residence/construction and improvement of residential buildings	1.8	2.6	3.1	2.7	6.9	11.8
Purchase of land for business and other purposes/construction and improvement of other buildings	0.6	0.0	1.0	0.0	0.9	0.4
Investment in farm/business	5.2	1.6	1.9	0.0	9.1	1.1
Deposits and stocks	0.0	0.0	2.2	4.1	0.0	0.0
Education	10.3	10.8	1.8	1.4	23.1	17.3
Household goods	41.4	13.4	0.6	0.0	31.9	44.5
Food and clothing	40.5	40.8	80.7	77.0	23.3	23.5
Repayment of debts	0.2	0.8	6.4	13.5	0.6	1.1
Others	0.0	0.0	2.9	1.4	4.3	0.4
All	100.0	100.0	100.0	100.0	100.0	100.0

two states. In Uttar Pradesh the situation is slightly better, with remittances accounting for almost 50 per cent of the total income of out-migrant households in the bottom three income deciles. As regards the distribution of total remittances among the different income decile groups, the data show that the bottom three deciles of the out-migrant households receive almost half the total remittances, whereas the share of the top three is about one-fifth.

Table 4.6 shows the effect of remittances on the level and distribution of incomes of out-migrant households. The figures suggest that remittances raise the average income of out-migrant households in Bihar, Kerala and Uttar Pradesh by 47.8, 73.8 and 25.1 per cent respectively. Remittances not only raise the level of income of out-migrant households, they also significantly improve the distribution of income in out-migrant households. The data show that there is a decline in the Gini coefficient of about 20 per cent in Bihar and Uttar Pradesh, and in Kerala the figure is even higher (36.2 per cent). This shows that the distribution of income tends to become more egalitarian when remittances are included. In other words, the relative effect of remittances is much greater on poorer households and therefore helps to reduce the gap between the bottom and the top income groups.

The multiple regression results for the determinants of remittances are presented in table 4.7. In the case of Bihar, the results indicate that heads of households, as well as children of the household head, are more likely to send remittances than other relatives. This is understandable since the household head and the children are under a greater obligation to provide for the needs of the family left behind. The same is true with regard to the size of remittances. The proportion of remitters is higher among the married than among the unmarried, although the size of remittances does not differ significantly between the two groups. This may be largely because some of the married out-migrants take their families with them and, consequently, are not able to send any more than the unmarried. With regard to education, although the proportion of remitters is not generally significantly different among the educated and uneducated, level of education does have a significant positive influence on the size of remittances. In other words, although education does not influence the decision to remit, it does affect the quantum of remittances. It is also interesting to note that the coefficients related to size of remittances increase with the level of education. This is largely because education is a proxy

Table 4.5: Remittances received by out-migrant households by level of household income

Income decile groups	No. of out-migrant households	% receiving remittances	Mean remittances (Rs)	Mean household income excluding remittances (Rs)	Remittances as % of Household income including remittances	Remittances as % of All remittances
Bihar						
1	151	89.5	2 267	189	92.6	21.9
2	125	76.2	2 116	796	73.1	17.0
3	109	67.0	1 838	1 270	59.1	12.8
4	83	53.6	1 192	1 726	40.8	6.4
5	81	56.8	1 438	2 100	40.6	7.4
6	84	54.8	1 366	2 558	34.8	7.3
7	72	47.3	1 364	3 188	29.9	6.4
8	82	45.1	1 199	4 084	22.7	6.3
9	91	43.6	1 305	5 649	18.4	7.8
10	83	34.5	1 219	16 575	6.7	6.8
All	961	60.1	1 617	3 381	31.7	100.0
Kerala						
1	150	98.0	6 516	597	92.4	25.0
2	102	89.8	5 639	1 767	76.3	15.3
3	67	84.9	4 845	2 997	61.4	8.9
4	50	85.5	3 784	4 142	43.5	5.2
5	53	70.2	5 088	5 179	49.7	7.3
6	58	75.4	5 219	6 377	44.8	8.5
7	59	62.1	3 037	7 993	28.2	5.0
8	60	66.7	5 484	10 364	29.9	9.5

9	56	81.2	4 418	13 883	24.3	7.6
10	65	57.5	3 894	26 865	12.5	7.8
All	720	79.7	5 066	6 860	41.0	100.0
Uttar Pradesh						
1	108	88.1	2 294	873	72.3	20.8
2	90	72.3	1 930	1 960	50.3	14.6
3	57	71.2	1 868	2 619	42.1	8.9
4	92	50.5	1 200	3 226	26.8	10.1
5	82	56.1	1 522	4 120	27.0	10.3
6	82	53.6	1 312	5 080	20.6	8.9
7	64	45.6	1 127	6 195	15.3	6.6
8	79	42.2	1 004	7 603	11.6	7.3
9	63	32.8	954	10 243	8.5	5.0
10	75	34.5	917	19 532	4.1	7.5
All	792	56.1	1 453	5 781	19.3	100.0

Note: Deciles refer to the income (excluding remittances) of all the households in the sample and not just the out-migrant household.

Table 4.6: Effect of remittances on level and distribution of incomes of out-migrant households

	No. of households	Income excluding remittances	Income including remittances	Percentage change in income/Gini coefficient
Mean household income				
Bihar	961	3 381	4 998	47.88
Kerala	720	6 860	11 926	73.8
Uttar Pradesh	792	5 781	7 234	25.1
Distribution of income (Gini coefficient)				
Bihar	961	0.547	0.431	21.2
Kerala	720	0.549	0.350	36.2
Uttar Pradesh	792	0.471	0.385	18.3

for income, and with increasing income the out-migrant's capacity to remit is also more. The present place of residence of out-migrants (rural or urban) does not have much impact either on the decision to remit or on the size of remittances. However, distance does influence the propensity to remit. The proportion of remitters as well as the size of remittances is higher among those who migrate outside the state. Further, it is clear that both the proportion of remitters and the amount of remittances increase with years since migration. As years since migration increase, the incomes of out-migrants also increase and so does their capacity to remit to support their poor families back home. It is also revealed that a low proportion of workers among the remaining household members is one of the most compelling reasons for out-migrants to remit. The coefficients of the variables related to per capita land and income, which also indicate the dependency of the origin household on remittances, have the expected sign, but turn out to be insignificant. However, when the dependency variable (proportion of workers among remaining household members) is excluded from the equation, the results, although not presented here, show that the proportion of remitters is significantly higher among households with lower incomes.

Multiple regression results for Kerala clearly indicate that although a larger proportion of sons and daughters remit than other relatives, they do not necessarily remit larger sums. Neither the proportion of remitters nor the size of remittances is influenced by education, except when the level of education is very high. Because Gulf migration is for fixed periods, the years since migration do not show any impact on the proportion of remitters but they do have a significant positive association with the size of remittances. Although the proportion of remitters decreases as a function of the size of landholding, the quantum of remittances increases. From among the variables indicating the dependency of the out-migrant households, per capita land and income have a significant negative relation with the decision to remit, whereas the proportion of workers remaining has a significant negative association and per capita land a significant positive association with the size of remittances. When the variable, per capita land, is excluded from the regression, per capita income again turns out to be significant, as in the case of Bihar, indicating that the propensity to remit is higher among out-migrants from poorer households.

The findings for Uttar Pradesh are somewhat different from those for Bihar and Kerala. The variables indicating the relationship of the out-migrant to the household head are significant for both Bihar and Kerala in explaining the decision to remit and the size of remittance, but in Uttar Pradesh they are not. The education variable has a significantly positive impact on the size of remittances only if the out-migrant has secondary level education. Present place of residence is again less relevant in Uttar Pradesh, except that out-migrants who go outside the state remit significantly more than those who remain within the state. The variable 'years since migration' has a significant positive effect on the size of remittances in both Bihar and Kerala, but no such effect is present in the case of Uttar Pradesh, although it is seen to be positively associated with the decision to remit. Finally, the variables relating to the need of the parent family (proportion of household members working, per capita land and income) appear to have some impact on the decision to remit, but no significant influence on the size of remittances, possibly because of the relatively higher level of agricultural development in Uttar Pradesh as compared to the other two states.

Table 4.7: Estimated regression equations for the determinants of remittances from rural out-migrants (Dependent variables: proportion of remitters; size of remittances) (t-values are given in brackets)

Independent variables		Bihar		Kerala		Uttar Pradesh	
		Proportion of remitters	Size of remittances	Proportion of remitters	Size of remittances	Proportion of remitters	Size of remittances
HEAD	1 if head of household; 0 otherwise	0.210** (5.02)	0.645** (3.41)	0.342** (7.46)	2.309** (4.51)	0.161 (0.72)	−3.469 (0.62)
SNDT	1 if son or daughter; 0 otherwise	0.124*** (3.32)	0.414** (2.34)	0.166** (4.98)	(0.222) (0.53)	(.013) (0.29)	−3.490** (2.56)
OTHR	1 if other relations of head; 0 otherwise	—	—	—	—	—	—
MRRD	1 if married; 0 otherwise	0.062+ (1.72)	0.213 (1.22)	−0.036 (1.26)	0.169 (0.50)	0.117** (2.74)	1.463 (1.09)
EDN1	1 if with no formal education; 0 otherwise	—	—	—	—	—	—
EDN2	1 if education is less than secondary; 0 otherwise	0.075** (2.40)	0.323** (2.40)	—	—	—	—
EDN3	1 if education is secondary; 0 otherwise	0.064 (1.50)	0.938** (5.10)	0.042 (1.43)	0.226 (0.66)	0.005 (0.13)	4.241** (3.36)
EDN4	1 if education is graduation or above; 0 otherwise	0.044 (0.50)	1.375** (3.51)	0.128** (2.74)	1.619** (2.95)	−0.031 (0.54)	1.273 (0.67)
URBN	1 if out-migrant to urban areas; 0 otherwise	0.005 (0.15)	−0.002 (0.01)	0.168** (5.33)	0.119 (0.30)	−0.009 (0.18)	−2.001 (1.32)
OSTA	1 if out-migrant to outside the state; 0 otherwise	0.055+ (1.67)	0.249+ (1.66)	0.219** (7.24)	6.108** (18.29)	0.029 (0.77)	5.417** (4.67)

YRSM	Years since migration	0.018** (5.16)	0.066** (4.48)	0.001 (0.16)	0.009* (2.20)	0.014** (2.70)	0.016 (1.01)
PHMW	Percentage of household members working	−0.003** (4.60)	−0.010** (3.62)	−0.001 (1.44)	−0.003** (3.34)	0.002* (2.17)	−0.002 (0.61)
LAND	Amount of per capita land	−0.002 (0.09)	−0.011 (0.09)	−0.003** (3.48)	−0.004** (4.04)	−0.228** (5.07)	−2.833 (1.51)
PCIN	Per capita income of parent family excluding remittances (in thousand rupees)	−0.011 (1.12)	−0.002 (0.04)	−0.033 (3.26)	0.180 (1.24)	−0.002 (0.11)	0.644 (0.97)
	Constant	0.423	0.868	0.467	0.941	0.505	6.091
	R²	0.154	0.156	0.219	0.442	0.144	0.130
	F	14.630	10.856	24.026	54.812	8.780	5.234
	(N)	(978)	(717)	(1,042)	(774)	(587)	(398)

Notes: Coefficients of the regression for size of remittances are in 10^3.

** Significant at 1 per cent level.
* Significant at 5 per cent level.
+ Significant at 10 per cent level.

CHAPTER 5

MIGRATION, PRODUCTION AND TECHNOLOGICAL CHANGE IN AGRICULTURE

Migration from rural areas involves information and income flows as well as human resource flows. All these are likely to influence agricultural production and technology. The present chapter, therefore, attempts to analyse the relationship between migration and agricultural development. The methodology adopted is to compare the adoption of technology and land and labour productivity in migrant and non-migrant households.

The distribution of households by landholding category for different migration status groups, given in table 5.1, shows that the amount of land held by out-migrant and return-migrant households is not very different from that held by non-migrant households in any of the three states. It cannot, therefore, be maintained that, in any of the states, households from a particular landholding category are over-represented in the migration stream. It should be noted, however, that the largest proportion of households in rural areas in each of the three states belongs to the category of holdings up to 2.5 acres, about 62, 94 and 54 per cent in Bihar, Kerala and Uttar Pradesh respectively.

Although there is no significant difference in the distribution of landholdings between migrant and non-migrant households, differences in the degree of their adoption of improved implements, new technology, etc., could lead to an assessment as to whether migration has any possible favourable impact on agricultural progress. The data presented in table 5.2 in general show that in the case of wheat, HYV (high yielding variety) is being used by a relatively larger proportion of households in Bihar (83 per cent) than in Uttar Pradesh (55.7 per cent). The relatively higher proportion of adopters in Bihar is due to the fact that the estimates relate to Saran district where agriculture is not so backward. In the other district in our sample

**Table 5.1: Percentage distribution of cultivating households by
landholding and migration status**

Landholding	Type of household			
category	Out-migrant	Return-migrant	Non-migrant	All
Bihar				
(N)	(560)	(122)	(464)	(1 146)
Up to 2.5 acres	60.9	60.7	64.5	62.3
2.6–5.0 acres	22.8	23.0	19.6	21.2
5.1–10.0 acres	11.5	13.9	9.7	11.0
10+ acres	4.8	2.5	6.3	5.2
Kerala				
(N)	(501)	(207)	(606)	(1 314)
Up to 2.5 acres	92.6	92.8	96.5	94.4
2.6–5.0 acres	5.8	5.8	2.3	4.2
5.1–10.0 acres	1.6	1.0	1.0	1.2
10+ acres	0.0	0.5	0.2	0.2
Uttar Pradesh				
(N)	(477)	(131)	(506)	(1 114)
Up to 2.5 acres	49.9	61.8	56.4	54.2
2.6–5.0 acres	26.0	27.5	24.7	25.6
5.1–10.0 acres	16.9	9.2	11.5	13.6
10+ acres	7.1	1.5	7.3	6.6

(Singhbhum), wheat is not grown. In the case of rice, the highest
proportion of adopters (57.6 per cent) is found in Kerala, followed
by Uttar Pradesh (31.1 per cent). With regard to migrant status,
return-migrant households show a larger proportion of adopters
than the other two categories for most crops in the three states. Out-
migrant households also show a larger proportion than non-migrants
for wheat and maize in Bihar, coconut in Kerala, and rice in Uttar
Pradesh. But it should be noted that in none of the three states are
the differences between out-migrant, return-migrant and non-migrant
households very large.

The adoption of modern agricultural technology such as the use
of a tractor, thresher and tubewell may also be positively affected by
remittances. Migration flows are not only carriers of information
but also of capital and income, as noted earlier. They can therefore
have a significant impact on the use of costly modern technology. In
the case of poor rural Bihar (table 5.3), it seems that remittances
associated with out-migration have certainly helped promote the

Table 5.2: Percentage of farming households that have grown HYV crops by migration status

State/crops	Type of household			
	Out-migrant	Return-migrant	Non-migrant	All
Bihar				
Wheat	84.0	91.4	79.4	83.0
Maize	70.5	50.0	58.7	62.8
Rice	13.2	18.5	14.2	14.1
Kerala				
Coconut	11.2	15.8	9.3	10.8
Rice	52.7	61.4	60.0	57.6
Uttar Pradesh				
Wheat	53.5	59.4	56.9	55.7
Rice	32.0	32.3	29.7	31.1

use of costly implements for agricultural progress. The limited use of threshers and still more limited use of tractors indicate the unsuitable character of these implements in an area where there is a predominance of small farmers. But the highest proportions of tractor-, thresher- and tubewell-using households are in the category of out-migrant households receiving remittances. The breakdown of data by farm size, although not presented here, reveals that among out-migrant households receiving remittances it is mostly the small farmers who are making greater use of modern implements as compared with non-migrant and return-migrant households. This shows that remittances do enable poor farming households to shift to modern technology, perhaps both to increase their agricultural output and to compensate for the labour lost due to out-migration of one or more of their members. It is also worth noting that the second greatest users of threshers and tubewells are the return-migrant households.

In Uttar Pradesh, the scenario is altogether different. Though out-migrant households are the greatest users of modern implements, it is those among them who do not receive remittances who show by far the highest levels of use, and this pattern persists for each farm-size class. Remittances thus do not seem to promote the use of these costly implements in Uttar Pradesh. This may be because the remittances are being received by the poorer households or because those receiving remittances are using them for the purchase of land and other assets rather than to buy modern implements. There is some evidence of this as noted earlier in Chapter 4. The second highest proportion of users was found among the non-migrant households (for tractors and threshers) and among return-migrant households (for tubewells). The pattern of use of tractors and tubewells in Kerala (though at lower levels) is similar to that of Uttar Pradesh.

Table 5.3: Percentage of cultivating households using modern agricultural technology by migration status

States/agricultural technology	Type of household				
	Out-migrant		Return-migrant	Non-migrant	All
	Receiving remittances	Not receiving remittances			
Bihar					
Tractor	4.6	1.6	1.6	2.6	2.8
Thresher	20.2	2.4	13.9	11.0	11.9
Tubewell	30.6	7.1	25.4	19.6	20.4
Kerala					
Tractor	3.5	19.6	8.2	2.8	5.1
Thresher	0.0	0.0	0.0	0.0	0.0
Tubewell	12.9	39.2	21.7	23.1	20.9
Uttar Pradesh					
Tractor	9.8	33.3	7.6	10.7	13.3
Thresher	7.9	33.3	6.8	9.3	12.0
Tubewell	16.4	34.6	25.2	18.4	20.9

The data on average household expenditure on fertilizer and HYV seed presented in table 5.4 present a similar pattern. In the case of Bihar, out-migrant households receiving remittances spend more on fertilizer and HYV seed than non-migrant households. In Kerala and Uttar Pradesh, on the other hand, all out-migrant households (both receiving and not receiving remittances) spend relatively more on these inputs than non-migrant households, with those not receiving remittances spending more than those receiving remittances. In all three states, return-migrant households spend more on these inputs than non-migrant households.

Modern agricultural practices like seed treatment, weed control

Table 5.4: Average household expenditure on fertilizer and HYV seed by migration status

States	Type of household				
	Out-migrant		Return-migrant	Non-migrant	All
	Receiving remittances	Not receiving remittances			
Bihar	132	67	128	104	106
Kerala	299	616	557	258	344
Uttar Pradesh	781	1 007	757	750	797

and plant protection are generally least popular in Bihar, where agriculture is at its lowest level of development, and most popular in Uttar Pradesh, which has the most developed agriculture among the three states (table 5.5). Kerala's level, so far as these practices are concerned, is almost as low as that in Bihar. Though the variation in the proportion of households using these techniques is not great among different migration status groups, it is nevertheless true that the proportion of households using these techniques is generally higher in the case of out-migrant and return-migrant households taken together.

Table 5.5: Percentage of cultivating households using modern agricultural practices by migration status

State/farm practices	Type of household			
	Out-migrant	Return-migrant	Non-migrant	All
Bihar				
Seed treatment	3.8	2.5	3.2	3.4
Weed control	5.7	7.4	5.4	5.8
Plant protection	8.8	13.9	10.3	9.9
Kerala				
Seed treatment	1.2	1.0	1.2	1.1
Weed control	6.2	8.2	5.4	6.2
Plant protection	18.4	27.1	18.2	19.6
Uttar Pradesh				
Seed treatment	43.8	41.9	39.4	41.6
Weed control	89.9	83.2	85.9	87.3
Plant protection	43.0	42.0	31.9	37.8

However, even if a relatively higher proportion of migrant households are using HYV seed-fertilizer technology, modern implements and improved agricultural practices, it is not clear whether their adoption had preceded or followed migration. Table 5.6 gives the percentage of out-migrant households who adopted HYV seeds and modern technology since migration. The data show that, in the case of Bihar and Uttar Pradesh, the majority of out-migrant households adopted the modern technology after migration, which may suggest that migration does contribute towards promoting the use of new agricultural technology. In the case of Kerala, however, the adoption of modern agricultural technology appears to have largely preceded, rather than followed, migration except in the case of coconut. This may be because of the generally higher levels of education and greater awareness of new agricultural techniques even before one or more household members out-migrated.

Table 5.6: Percentage of out-migrant households who have adopted HYV and modern technology since migration

HYV/modern technology	Bihar	Kerala	Uttar Pradesh
HYV			
Wheat*	62.1	90.1	61.9
Maize	58.1	—	—
Rice	66.7	39.4	—
Modern technology			
Tractor	65.0	34.3	56.0
Thresher	72.2	—	86.7
Tubewell	64.6	33.3	57.7

* For Kerala this refers to coconut.

The use of HYV seed-fertilizer technology requires complementary inputs such as irrigation. But it should be noted that the use of irrigation does not depend on the farmer's own effort alone; it also depends greatly on efficient water management and the availability of irrigation infrastructure and credit.

Table 5.7 presents data on the use of irrigation by migrant and non-migrant households. The data, in general, show that whereas, in Uttar Pradesh, nearly all households are using some source of irrigation, only about two-thirds and one-third of households in Bihar and Kerala respectively are doing so. The use of tubewells, a nontraditional source of irrigation, is, however, much lower in all three states, as noted earlier in table 5.3. This perhaps indicates that the infrastructural support (e.g. power and institutional credit) is weak in the rural areas of all three states. The overall low level of irrigation in both Kerala and Bihar further indicates that the infrastructural support in these two states is probably even weaker, which must act as a drag on agricultural progress. It also emerges from table 5.7 that the process of out-migration and return-migration in rural areas, associated with remittances, does help promote the use of irrigation among cultivating households. In all three states, the proportion of households using irrigation is higher among return-migrants than among non-migrants, more prominently in Bihar. The proportion of households using some source of irrigation is also higher among out-migrant households receiving remittances than among those not receiving remittances or non-migrant households in both Bihar and Uttar Pradesh. Thus we find considerable evidence to support the hypothesis that the process of migration, through the inflow of resources and information, has promoted the use of irrigation in agriculture, the most important source of livelihood for the rural population.

Table 5.7: Percentage of cultivating households using irrigation

Type of household	Bihar	Kerala	Uttar Pradesh
Out-migrant households receiving remittances	70.1	25.3	98.6
Out-migrant households not receiving remittances	48.8	59.1	98.2
All out-migrant households	60.6	31.9	98.5
Return-migrant households	75.4	35.2	99.2
Non-migrant households	58.8	34.8	97.0
All	61.4	33.7	97.9
(N)	(1 154)	(1 151)	(1 053)

Although migration does seem to have some positive influence on the adoption of modern agricultural technology, it is important to examine whether and to what extent there are significant differences in land productivity between migrant and non-migrant households. The data given in table 5.8 show that in all three states, the value of gross output per acre of operational holding is higher for out-migrant and return-migrant than for non-migrant households. Between the two types of migrant households, the return-migrant households show even better performance than the out-migrant households. Indeed, the percentage difference in land productivity between return-migrant and non-migrant households is as high as 33 and 39 in Kerala and Uttar Pradesh respectively. The relatively higher level of productivity among return-migrants may be because they bring both resources and information to their places of origin.

Table 5.8: Agricultural output by migration status

	Type of household			
	Out-migrant	Return-migrant	Non-migrant	All
Bihar (N = 1,154)				
Gross value of agricultural output per acre (Rs)	611	621	557	590
Index of gross value of output per acre*	110	111	100	106
Kerala (N = 1,151)				
Gross value of agricultural output per acre (Rs)	3 883	5 021	3 772	4 059
Index of gross value of output per acre*	103	133	100	108
Uttar Pradesh (N = 1,053)				
Gross value of agricultural output per acre (Rs)	2 374	3 009	2 163	2 322
Index of gross value of output per acre*	110	139	100	107

* Non-migrant households taken as base = 100.

The positive effect of migration on the adoption of modern technology and land productivity is also likely to have secondary effects in both the agricultural and the non-agricultural sectors of the rural economy. Such effects are most likely to be felt in terms of changes in the levels of employment and earnings. In a labour surplus situation, the level of employment, measured in terms of person-days per worker, is likely to increase with out-migration and the associated flow of remittances. This is because while the out-migration per se will decrease the number of workers both in out-migrant family and in the out-migration area in general, the associated remittances will probably help raise the level of productive capital in the rural economy.

In the case of return-migration, however, the effect on employment is difficult to judge a priori, since there would be an inflow of both labour and capital.

Table 5.9 presents information about employment and workers' earnings in migrant and non-migrant households. The figures show that there is a distinct improvement in the employment situation in Kerala, both in the out-migrant and return-migrant households, as compared to non-migrant ones. The number of person-days employed per worker is highest among workers in return-migrant households. This perhaps suggests that return-migrant households have a relatively higher inflow of resources and possibly better information to enable them to use those resources more efficiently. In Uttar Pradesh, there is no evidence of any increase in employment. In Bihar, on the other hand, the number of person-days employed per worker in out-migrant households is actually lower than that for non-migrant households, perhaps because a larger proportion of the active members of the out-migrant households have left, leaving behind relatively more

Table 5.9: Employment and earnings of workers by migration status*

	Type of household			
	Out-migrant	*Return-migrant*	*Non-migrant*	*All*
Bihar (N = 2,025)				
Person-days employed per worker in a year	209	210	224	217
Earnings per employed person-day (Rs)	.11.9	10.5	9.3	10.4
Kerala (N = 1742)				
Person-days employed per worker in a year	302	310	289	296
Earnings per employed person-day (Rs)	23.4	27.7	19.9	22.1
Uttar Pradesh (N = 1874)				
Person-days employed per worker in a year	300	287	300	298
Earnings per employed person-day (Rs)	13.3	14.6	14.0	13.8

* Figures refer to workers in both agricultural and non-agricultural households in the rural sample.

workers in the younger and older age groups.

As regards earnings per employed person-day, these are in general lowest in Bihar and highest in Kerala. In all three states, earnings are higher for workers in return-migrant households than for those in non-migrant households. In Bihar and Kerala, earnings are also higher for workers in out-migrant households than for workers in non-migrant households; in Uttar Pradesh, however, earnings are almost equal for these two groups of workers. The earning differentials between workers in migrant and non-migrant households may be due to two reasons. First, both out-migrant and return-migrant households may have a relatively higher capital-labour ratio because of remittances. Second, increased levels of consumption in migrant households, made possible by remittances, may contribute towards the higher labour productivity of their workers.

Yet another aspect of the impact of migration on the employment situation relates to whether the loss of labour in out-migrant households is compensated for by employing additional hired labour and/or by increasing the participation rates of female members of the household. The relevant data in this respect are presented in table 5.10, which shows clearly that, in all three states, the loss of labour arising from out-migration is partly compensated for by employing more hired labour in cultivation and partly by increased participation of females in work. Among the return-migrant households, however, the pattern of use of either hired labour or female labour is not uniform. In Bihar, the use of both hired labour and female labour is relatively lower among return-migrant households. This may be due both to the increase in family labour after the return of the migrant and to the increased work effort of household members. In Uttar Pradesh, return-migrant households have a relatively higher level of use of both hired and female labour as compared with out-migrant and non-migrant households. This is partly because a relatively large proportion of return-migrants in Uttar Pradesh are using HYV seed-fertilizer technology, which requires more labour, and partly because many of the return-migrants are retired people, whose dependence on hired labour is relatively more. In Kerala, the fact that the use of hired labour is the highest and of female labour the lowest among return-migrant households probably suggests that the return-migrants there bring back enough resources to enable them to use more hired labour in place of female labour. This is quite likely in view of the fact that many of the return-

**Table 5.10: Use of hired and female labour by
type of household**

	Type of household			
	Out-migrant	Return-migrant	Non-migrant	All
Bihar				
Hired labour person-days per acre (mean for agricultural households)	6.0	2.8	4.2	4.9
Percentage of female workers to total workers in agricultural households	33.9 (36.5)	26.0 (27.8)	27.3 (31.0)	30.1 (32.8)
Kerala				
Hired labour person-days per acre (mean for agricultural households)	47.8	65.4	43.2	49.5
Percentage of female workers to total workers in agricultural households	15.0 (16.3)	11.9 (13.6)	14.8 (16.2)	14.2 (15.8)
Uttar Pradesh				
Hired labour person-days per acre (mean for agricultural households)	21.8	24.3	15.7	19.1
Percentage of female workers to total workers in agricultural households	42.4 (34.5)	43.2 (37.3)	37.4 (25.3)	40.4 (30.3)

Note: Figures in brackets refer to both agricultural and non-agricultural households.

migrants in Kerala went to the Gulf countries for work.

Table 5.11 presents the results of stepwise regressions for the determinants of land productivity. The independent variables considered were per capita land, intensity of cropping, fertilizer consumption per acre, proportion of area under high yielding varieties, hired labour (person-days) per acre, proportion of wage/salary earners in the household, and three dummy variables representing irrigation use, remittance-receiving and return-migrant households. In addition, slope dummies, representing the interaction of the three dummy variables with the rest, were also considered. Some of these variables did not, however, turn out to be significant in any of the three equations and are therefore not included in the final results presented in the table.

In the case of Bihar, the results indicate that the phenomena of return-migration and remittances, each coupled with the practice of double/multiple cropping, significantly contribute towards higher land productivity. Though the association between land productivity and fertilizer consumption per acre is expectedly positive, the effect is lower in the case of return-migrant households. This is probably explained by the fact that the intensity of cropping is much higher for return-migrant households and, consequently, fertilizer consumption per cropped acre is lower. Thus, even though land productivity increases with fertilizer consumption per acre, the proportionate increase in land productivity is less than the proportionate increase in fertilizer consumption in the case of return-migrant households. In the case of Kerala, return-migrant households that are also using more hired labour and fertilizer are able to increase land productivity, probably because of better supervision.

In Uttar Pradesh, as in Bihar, fertilizer use has a positive association with land productivity. The phenomena of return-migration and remittances, each coupled with a greater use of fertilizer, cause a significant increase in land productivity. As regards the use of hired labour, this is seen to have a significant positive relationship with land productivity in Kerala and Uttar Pradesh, but not in Bihar. This is possibly because of the dominance of semi-feudal modes of production in Bihar's agriculture. Irrigation, interacting with per capita land, shows a positive effect on land productivity in Kerala, whereas its positive effect on land productivity in Bihar is only realized when interacting with intensity of cropping. Because of the very high percentage of irrigation users (about 98 per cent) in Uttar Pradesh, its impact could not be discerned when a dummy variable for use of irrigation was used. The negative relationship between per capita land productivity and landholding in Kerala and Uttar Pradesh and between land productivity and interaction of landholding and irrigation in Bihar may suggest that the level of agricultural technology is low in all three states. However, the positive role of migration flows towards improving the general level of land and labour productivity in the rural areas can hardly be denied.

Table 5.11: Estimated stepwise regressions for the determinants of gross value of agricultural output per acre
(t-values are given in brackets)

Independent variables	Bihar	Kerala	Uttar Pradesh
Intensity of cropping	8.250** (15.52)	30.181** (14.80)	7.074** (3.59)
Fertilizer consumption per acre	6.604** (15.47)	—	0.855** (9.90)
Proportion of wage earners among labour force	−127.442** (2.69)	—	—
Interaction, irrigation dummy and fertilizer consumption per acre	−4.343** (9.52)	—	—
Interaction, irrigation dummy intensity of cropping	2.552** (6.38)	−24.751** (9.06)	—
Interaction, irrigation dummy and per capita landholding	−175.914** (4.44)	1,281.69** (2.13)	—
Interaction, return-migrant dummy and fertilizer consumption per acre	−3.240** (6.31)	0.614** (2.87)	0.676** (4.31)
Interaction, return-migrant dummy and intensity of cropping	1.271* (2.32)	—	—
Interaction, remittances dummy and intensity of cropping	0.604 (2.56)**	—	—
Hired labour per acre	—	19.332** (9.56)	19.815** (7.24)
Per capita landholding	—	−1,686.04** (3.42)	−843.585** (4.72)
Irrigation dummy	—	1,831.18** (6.09)	—
Remittances dummy	—	−464.38** (2.48)	—
Interaction, return migrant dummy and hired labour per acre	—	9.129** (3.21)	−16.886* (2.19)
Interaction, remittances dummy and fertilizer consumption per acre	—	—	0.409** (3.99)
Interaction, remittances dummy and proportion of wage earners	—	—	−1,517.68** (2.84)
Interaction, remittances dummy and per capita land	—	—	−1,238.96** (2.49)

Table 5.11 (*Contd.*)

Independent variables	Bihar	Kerala	Uttar Pradesh
Constant	−415.902	839.621	2,305.101
R^2	0.612	0.377	0.437
F	196.100**	76.586**	89.089**
(N)	(1 129)	(1 149)	(1 042)

Note: ** significant at 1 per cent level.
* significant at 5 per cent level.

CHAPTER 6

CHARACTERISTICS OF URBAN IN-MIGRANTS

Migrants may contribute to the growth of the urban economy through increased supply of unskilled and semi-skilled labour, greater labour productivity, higher incomes and diversification of industry and services. On the other hand, they may simply burden the urban economy through increased unemployment and underemployment, lower levels of productivity, and a greater demand for urban services. The net economic impact of in-migration on the urban areas will largely depend on the characteristics of the migrants involved. The purpose of this section is to examine the characteristics of the in-migrants as well as the differences between them and the natives, using the data gathered from the urban household surveys in the three states. Persons who in-migrated on account of job transfer are excluded from the analysis.

The data presented in table 6.1 show that the in-migrants in all three states are predominantly young adults. More than two-thirds belong to the 20–44 age group. The corresponding proportion for non-migrants is less than half. This shows the age selectivity of the migration process, although part of the difference may be due to the fact that children of in-migrants who were less than 10 years of age at the time of migration were not defined as in-migrants for the purpose of this study. As regards education, although the proportion of those who have no formal education is considerably lower in Kerala than in either Bihar or Uttar Pradesh, this proportion is lower among in-migrants than among non-migrants. The data, therefore, suggest that in general the educational level of in-migrants in Bihar and Kerala is higher than that of non-migrants, while in Uttar Pradesh the pattern is reversed. In Bihar, this may be partly because of the requirements of Bokaro industry for semi-skilled and skilled labour. In Kerala, the overall educational level of the population being generally high, it may require even greater selectivity with respect to education for

Table 6.1: Percentage distribution of urban in-migrants and non-migrants by sex, age and education

	Bihar		Kerala		Uttar Pradesh	
	In-migrants	*Non-migrants*	*In-migrants*	*Non-migrants*	*In-migrants*	*Non-migrants*
(N)	(1815)	(6047)	(1191)	(6075)	(968)	(5921)
Sex						
Male	52.1	56.9	51.8	49.5	70.0	52.5
Female	47.9	43.1	48.2	50.5	30.0	47.5
Age (years)						
10–19	8.4	41.3	12.2	27.9	7.6	30.9
20–44	80.9	41.9	71.6	45.9	82.8	48.2
45 +	10.7	17.8	16.2	26.2	9.5	20.9
Education						
No formal education	*21.2*	*21.6*	*2.4*	*4.8*	*27.0*	*17.9*
within 20–44 age group	19.7	25.8	1.2	2.1	26.8	16.9
Less than secondary	*39.5*	*48.9*	*35.1*	*60.3*	*29.8*	*37.7*
Within 20–44 age group	37.5	35.5	25.7	48.6	28.9	27.9
Secondary	*24.7*	*21.7*	*40.7*	*24.1*	*26.1*	*29.0*
Within 20–44 age group	25.7	25.2	45.0	13.0	25.6	30.8
Graduate and above	*14.5*	*7.7*	*21.8*	*10.7*	*17.0*	*15.4*
Within 20–44 age group	17.1	13.5	28.2	18.8	18.5	24.6

migrants to succeed in urban labour markets.

In-migrants to urban areas come from both rural and other urban areas. It is important, therefore, to examine whether or not there are significant differences in the demographic and socio-economic characteristics of those coming from rural areas and those from urban areas. Table 6.2 presents information about such possible differences for the three states. In Bihar and Kerala, the proportion of in-migrants in the 10–19 age group (the youngest age group) is higher for those who come from urban areas than for those from rural areas. It seems that the youngest persons from rural areas are perhaps less prone to migrate than those from urban areas. In Bihar and Kerala, there is not much rural-urban difference for the older age groups of more than 45 years. But in Uttar Pradesh, this group shows a higher proportion of in-migrants in the case of those coming from urban areas. Since the level of education is usually lower in rural areas, rural-urban migration streams have a higher proportion of people without formal education than urban-urban migration streams.

The proportion of females among in-migrants from urban areas is higher than that from rural areas for all three states. However, the proportion of females among in-migrants from rural areas is particularly low in the case of Uttar Pradesh as compared with the other two states. The feudal ethôs which operates as a drag on female migration is, thus, most evident in Uttar Pradesh. Married persons dominate the migration stream in all three states; in Bihar this dominance is more prominent in the case of in-migrants from rural than from urban areas, but this is not in the case in Kerala or Uttar Pradesh.

As regards activity status before migration, in all three states the percentage of 'students' remains higher among those coming from urban than from rural areas. A large proportion of in-migrants from rural areas were in the labour force before migration as compared to in-migrants from urban areas. This pattern is consistent with the hypothesis that rural-urban migration is influenced more by income differentials and employment prospects than urban-urban migration.

While in Bihar almost all the in-migrants from rural areas are either landless or own less than 2.5 acres of land, in Uttar Pradesh inmigrants are drawn from all landowning categories. The pattern in Kerala is similar to that in Bihar, but there agricultural landholdings are generally small. Thus, it is clear that the poor dominate the urban in-migration flow in Bihar.

The reason for migration given by the highest proportion of inmigrants, particularly from urban areas, was 'following or accompanying the family' in all three states. In Kerala and Uttar Pradesh, the search for employment/better employment is more pronounced for in-migrants from rural areas. The proportion who come for educational reasons is higher among in-migrants from rural areas than those from urban areas. This is because the rural areas generally do not have adequate facilities for further or good quality education. It is also interesting to note that in Kerala, the proportion of in-migrants coming from rural areas for educational reasons is somewhat lower than that in Bihar and Uttar Pradesh, reflecting the comparatively better educational facilities available in the rural areas of Kerala.

The data on 'years since migration' show that, in Kerala, the

**Table 6.2: Percentage distribution of urban in-migrants by
previous place of residence and demographic and
socio-economic characteristics**

Characteristics	Bihar		Kerala		Uttar Pradesh	
	Rural	Urban	Rural	Urban	Rural	Urban
(N)	(1 145)	(647)	(474)	(465)	(805)	(341)
Age (Years)						
10–19	24.4	26.3	19.6	21.7	31.3	26.1
20–44	67.1	64.5	71.3	67.6	65.2	67.1
45 +	8.4	9.2	9.1	10.7	3.5	6.8
Education						
No formal education	31.1	18.2	3.6	0.9	32.9	18.5
Less than secondary	40.2	43.4	42.1	34.1	33.2	30.8
Secondary	19.0	21.2	36.4	41.2	14.1	15.5
Graduate and above	9.7	17.2	18.0	23.9	19.8	35.2
Sex						
Male	57.0	43.3	60.3	43.2	74.0	58.9
Female	43.0	56.7	39.7	56.8	26.0	41.1
Marital status						
Married	71.7	65.0	51.2	60.8	68.7	67.7
Unmarried	19.5	24.1	43.8	34.3	29.6	28.4
Others	8.8	10.9	5.1	5.0	1.7	3.8
Activity status before migration						
Employed	14.2	11.2	34.3	22.1	31.5	27.3
Unemployed	28.6	15.7	25.0	13.1	24.0	16.1
Student	38.8	48.6	22.2	39.8	23.9	32.0
Others	18.4	24.4	18.4	25.0	20.7	24.7
Land owned in previous place						
None	31.5	72.0	67.7	84.3	60.6	92.9
Up to 2.5 acres	68.3	28.0	30.8	15.1	7.0	1.8
2.6–5.0 acres	0.0	0.0	1.1	0.6	11.2	2.1
5.0 + acres	0.2	0.0	0.4	0.0	21.3	3.3
Reasons for migration						
For employment/better employment	43.8	26.3	48.7	29.2	54.7	38.7
Education	7.9	5.9	5.9	3.4	9.2	3.2
Follow/accompany family	48.3	67.9	31.4	60.6	26.5	43.1
Others	0.0	0.0	14.0	6.8	9.6	15.0
Years since migration						
0–4	24.5	26.4	40.8	54.8	29.4	36.7
5–9	34.2	38.3	33.6	29.2	40.1	40.2
10 +	41.3	35.2	25.6	15.9	30.4	23.2

percentage of in-migrants from both rural and urban areas in recent years (0–4 years) is significantly higher than in the earlier periods. This perhaps indicates that the sizeable international migration from Kerala in recent years has had a positive influence on the flow of internal migration within the state.

There is always a time lag between the arrival of in-migrants (who come looking for jobs) and their getting settled in their first job. This information provides a clue to the understanding of the employment situation in the urban labour market. Table 6.3 clearly indicates that urban in-migrants in Kerala are quickly absorbed in the urban labour market: 98 per cent of those in-migrating from urban areas and 94 per cent of those in-migrating from rural areas got their first job within three months. All the in-migrants (both from rural and urban areas) who did not have formal education got their first job within three months. All those in-migrating from urban areas and with less than secondary education got their first job in less than three months. Though the time lag for some of the educated in-migrants was a little longer, nearly all of them got their first job within a year. This implies that the labour market of urban Kerala has a relatively high labour absorption capacity and is probably also well organized. The labour markets of urban Uttar Pradesh and Bihar, on the other hand, appear to be performing less well. In Bihar, about 86 per cent of in-migrants from rural areas and 83 per cent of in-migrants from urban areas got their first job within six months, while the respective percentages for Uttar Pradesh are 83 and 74. In Bihar, among the in-migrants from rural areas, about 94 per cent of those with no formal education and 90 per cent of graduates got their first job within six months. The respective percentages for Uttar Pradesh are 84 and 81. In Uttar Pradesh, however, 88 per cent of in-migrants from rural areas with less than secondary education got their first job within six months. These percentages are mostly lower in the case of in-migrants from urban areas. This difference is perhaps due to the fact that in-migrants from rural areas generally have lower levels of education and experience and may, therefore, have lower job expectations. They may also have a greater need for income and, therefore, take up whatever jobs are available. In Uttar Pradesh, about 12 per cent of in-migrants from rural areas and 20 per cent from urban areas took more than a year to get their first jobs. The respective percentages for Bihar are 6 and 5. This suggests that the labour markets in both these states have a relatively lower absorptive capacity and are

**Table 6.3: Percentage distribution of in-migrants who looked
for work after migration by period of waiting for job,
level of education at arrival, and previous place
of residence**

State/previous place of residence/period of waiting for first job	No formal education	Less than secondary	Secondary	Graduate and above	All
	Education at arrival				
Bihar					
Rural					
1–3 months	85.2	68.4	63.9	75.0	73.0
4–6 months	9.0	12.8	16.3	15.4	13.1
7–12 months	3.4	10.7	10.5	5.8	8.3
More than 1 year	2.2	6.1	9.3	3.8	5.7
Urban					
1–3 months	53.3	65.9	60.0	82.4	67.5
4–6 months	20.0	18.2	13.3	11.8	15.4
7–12 months	26.7	9.1	16.7	5.0	12.2
More than 1 year	0.0	6.8	10.0	0.0	4.9
Kerala					
Rural					
1–3 months	100.0	96.1	92.0	91.5	93.7
4–6 months	0.0	1.9	4.0	3.4	3.0
7–12 months	0.0-	1.9	1.0	5.1	2.2
More than 1 year	0.0	0.0	3.0	0.0	1.1
Urban					
1–3 months	100.0	100.0	95.0	98.4	97.6
4–6 months	0.0	0.0	1.7	0.0	0.6
7–12 months	0.0	0.0	3.3	1.7	1.8
More than 1 year	0.0	0.0	0.0	0.0	0.0
Uttar Pradesh					
Rural					
1–3 months	70.8	69.7	58.9	61.1	66.6
4–6 months	13.3	18.6	16.4	19.4	16.8
7–12 months	4.2	4.1	2.7	6.9	4.4
More than 1 year	11.7	7.6	21.9	12.5	12.1
Urban					
1–3 months	63.2	61.3	60.7	52.5	58.5
4–6 months	15.8	19.4	21.4	7.5	15.3
7–12 months	0.0	6.5	0.0	12.5	5.9
More than 1 year	21.1	12.9	17.9	27.5	20.3

probably poorly organized. The long waiting time experienced by many in-migrants often adds to the lumpenization and criminalization of the urban centres.

The most important method of obtaining a job in Bihar is through friends and relatives, for all those with no formal education or less than secondary education (table 6.4). For graduates and those with secondary education, the major source is 'self-effort', which includes jobs obtained through either an advertisement or an employment exchange. The situation is similar in Kerala, but in Uttar Pradesh the dependence on friends and relatives for obtaining jobs does not lessen, with increasing level of education, as much as in Bihar and Kerala.

Table 6.4: Percentage distribution of in-migrants by education and source of obtaining first employment

State/source of obtaining first employment	Education on arrival				
	No formal education	Less than secondary	Secondary	Graduate and above	All
Bihar					
(N)	(91)	(190)	(131)	(120)	(532)
Friends/relatives	61.5	58.9	41.2	19.2	46.0
Self-effort	38.4	41.0	58.0	80.8	53.9
Others	0.0	0.0	0.8	0.0	0.1
Kerala					
(N)	(9)	(125)	(137)	(102)	(373)
Friends/relatives	44.5	48.0	27.0	20.6	32.7
Self-effort	33.4	39.2	69.4	76.5	60.3
Others	22.2	12.8	3.6	2.9	6.9
Uttar Pradesh					
(N)	(150)	(197)	(121)	(177)	(645)
Friends/relatives	58.7	59.4	54.5	36.7	52.1
Self-effort	38.0	38.6	38.8	52.0	42.1
Others	3.3	2.1	6.6	11.3	5.7

The migration flow arising out of the search for better employment prospects is expected to bring about a sharp change in the activity and employment status of in-migrants before and after migration. The change is likely to be reflected in a marked shift towards the activity status 'employed' as shown in table 6.5. However, care should be taken in the interpretation of such a shift in the context of 'students'. A student cannot remain a student for long, and a change

Table 6.5: Percentage of in-migrants employed by previous place of residence and activity status before migration

State/activity status before migration	Previous place of residence			
	Rural		Urban	
	Percentate employed soon after migration	Percentage employed currently	Percentage employed soon after migration	Percentage employed currently
Bihar				
Employed	71.9	94.3	65.7	98.6
Unemployed	62.2	91.6	57.1	91.8
Housekeeping	2.7	4.1	1.0	1.0
Student	14.2	33.0	9.7	23.6
Kerala				
Employed	73.1	96.4	59.1	92.5
Unemployed	67.4	89.6	50.9	94.5
Housekeeping	3.1	3.1	0.0	1.8
Student	23.7	51.8	7.9	34.9
Uttar Pradesh				
Employed	95.7	93.8	95.0	96.0
Unemployed	89.0	89.8	85.0	85.0
Housekeeping	2.9	4.8	0.0	2.7
Student	29.5	42.3	17.0	20.5

in his activity status over the course of time need not therefore be attributed to migration. In Bihar 9.7 per cent of students coming from urban areas were employed within six months after migration. The corresponding percentage for those coming from rural areas is 14.2. This higher rate of change in the activity status of students among rural-urban migration flows is in evidence in all three states. This is mainly because in rural areas, where surplus labour and unemployment are considerable, students do not find many opportunities to change to gainful employment. A similar logic is valid for the change of status from 'housekeeping' to 'employed', but the magnitude of such change is likely to be much less—an expectation which is borne out by the survey data. The data clearly show that in all three states, those who were unemployed before migration have significantly improved their position since migration, with the position tending to improve further with increasing duration of stay in the

Table 6.6: Percentage distribution of employed in-migrants by employment status before migration and at first job in the city and previous place of residence

State	Previous place of residence/employment status before migration	Employment status at first job in city		
		Self-employed	Wage/salary earners	All
Bihar	*Rural*			
	Self-employed	64.5	35.5	100.0
	Wage/salary earner	11.7	88.3	100.0
	Urban			
	Self-employed	76.7	23.3	100.0
	Wage/salary earner	14.5	85.5	100.0
Kerala	*Rural*			
	Self-employed	19.2	80.8	100.0
	Wage/salary earner	5.8	94.2	100.0
	Urban			
	Self-employed	78.6	21.4	100.0
	Wage/salary earner	7.1	92.9	100.0
Uttar Pradesh	*Rural*			
	Self-employed	23.1	76.9	100.0
	Wage/salary earner	10.2	89.8	100.0
	Urban			
	Self-employed	50.0	50.0	100.0
	Wage/salary earner	10.5	89.5	100.0

city, for in-migrants from both rural and urban areas.

The comparison of employment status before migration with that at first employment in the city (table 6.6) shows that in Kerala and Uttar Pradesh, though some wage/salary earners become self-employed, there is a marked shift in favour of wage-salary earning, in the case of in-migrants from both rural and urban areas. In Bihar, this shift is less marked. It is interesting to note that, among the self-employed from rural areas, a major proportion shifts to wage employment after migration, except in the case of Bihar. Among the self-employed from the urban areas, however, half or more remain self-employed after migration. This suggests that the self-employed in the smaller urban centres who have already built up some capital stock move to larger urban centres which offer a larger market and greater income opportunities.

Evaluation of the effects of in-migration on incomes is not as straightforward as with changes in activity or employment status. The price effect on income has been minimised in our analysis by taking into account income before migration and income soon after migration, results of which are presented in table 6.7. The effect of rural-urban price differentials could not, however, be eliminated. The results show that, of in-migrants who were employed before migration, about 10 per cent in Kerala, 16 per cent in Bihar, and 41 per cent in Uttar Pradesh suffered a decline in income. This may be because not all those who were employed before migration could afford to wait for suitable employment. Further, those with poor support might have opted for inferior jobs to begin with. But it is worth noting that almost three-quarters of in-migrants in Bihar and Kerala and about half in Uttar Pradesh experienced an increase in income soon after migration. In Bihar, almost 50 per cent of in-migrants from rural areas and 30 per cent of in-migrants from urban areas more than doubled their income. This again indicates that rural-urban income differentials are relatively larger in Bihar than in the other two states.

The proportion of in-migrants who brought money with them at the time of migration was lowest in Kerala and highest in Uttar Pradesh (table 6.8). In all three states relatively more in-migrants from rural areas brought money than those from urban areas. The

Table 6.7: Percentage distribution of in-migrants who were employed before and soon after migration by changes in their income

State/previous place of residence	Percentage change in income						
	Declined	No change	1–25	26-50	51–100	100 +	All
Bihar							
Rural	15.7	6.1	12.2	7.8	11.3	47.0	100.0
Urban	17.8	8.9	4.4	15.6	22.2	31.1	100.0
Kerala							
Rural	6.6	12.6	35.1	19.2	13.9	12.6	100.0
Urban	13.1	11.1	34.3	23.3	9.1	9.1	100.0
Uttar Pradesh							
Rural	40.7	9.5	13.2	4.2	17.5	14.8	100.0
Urban	42.3	8.5	13.4	3.4	16.7	15.7	100.0

Table 6.8: Money brought at the time of migration by recent (0–4 years' standing) in-migrants by employment status at first job and previous place of residence

Previous place of residence/ employment status at first job	Bihar		Kerala		Uttar Pradesh	
	Percentage of in-migrants who brought	Average amount per bringing in-migrant (Rs)	Percentage of in-migrants who brought	Average amount per bringing in-migrant (Rs)	Percentage of in-migrants who brought	Average amount per bringing in-migrant (Rs)
Rural						
(N)	(280)		(193)		(237)	
Self-employed	90.0	2 100	63.6	6 655	89.8	1 968
Wages/salary earner	88.5	386	59.8	1 920	91.9	778
Others	44.8	312	25.3	3 134	59.1	1 289
All	60.0	440	46.6	3 760	77.6	1 118
Urban						
(N)	(171)		(255)		(125)	
Self-employed	100.0	3 542	100.0	13 522	100.0	1 050
Wage/salary earner	96.3	691	69.5	5 885	92.9	1 926
Others	18.3	779	10.7	26 833	29.1	1 808
All	33.9	1 031	27.4	14 427	55.2	1 815

average amount brought was highest in Kerala and lowest in Bihar. In each case the average amount brought by in-migrants from urban areas was higher than that brought by in-migrants from rural areas. The average amount of money brought by the self-employed was almost always greater than that brought by wage/salary earners. Among the self-employed, however, those who came from urban areas brought relatively more money than those from rural areas, except in Uttar Pradesh. This is consistent with the earlier observation that some of the self-employed in the smaller urban centres are relocating their investments in larger urban centres. It is also interesting to note that in Kerala among in-migrants from urban areas who were not in the labour force after migration, although only one out of 10 brought money, the average amount brought was quite high (Rs 26833).

CHAPTER 7

MIGRATION AND
LABOUR FORCE PARTICIPATION

The labour force participation rate here indicates the proportion of the population aged 10 + in the workforce. In-migrants are likely to show a higher participation rate than non-migrants because the dominant reason for migration is looking for work and income. This difference is likely to be more pronounced in the younger age groups because non-migrants in this age group (unless very poor) would opt for education rather than work. In developing regions where migrants come relatively more from the poorer sections of society, in-migrants are likely to have higher participation rates, as participation rates are likely to be higher among the poor than among the rich. These hypotheses are confirmed by table 7.1. In each state, the participation rates both for the 10–24 age group and overall are higher for in-migrants than for non-migrants. As regards rural-urban differences, the participation rate is higher for in-migrants from rural areas than for those from urban areas (with the lone exception of the 60 + age group in Bihar). As regards sex, participation rates (taking all age groups together) are higher for both male and female in-migrants than for non-migrants in Bihar and Kerala, and for male in-migrants in Uttar Pradesh. Normally one would expect a person over 60 to be out of the labour force, unless the low-income syndrome compels him to continue working in the private sector or he is self-employed. The urban centres in Bihar and Uttar Pradesh, by and large, do suffer from the low-income syndrome. The participation rates of about 31 and 21 per cent respectively for in-migrants and non-migrants in the age group 60 and above in Uttar Pradesh may perhaps be due to greater absorption of workers in wage employment in the private sector, as noted in the subsequent section. It will be seen there that private sector wage employment accounts for 59 and 45 per cent of migrants and non-migrants respectively. In Bihar, the relatively high participation rates among the 60 + age group

**Table 7.1: Labour force participation rates by
age, sex, migration status and previous place of residence**

Age/sex/previous place of residence	Bihar		Kerala		Uttar Pradesh	
	In-migrants	Non-migrants	In-migrants	Non-migrants	In-migrants	Non-migrants
10–24 years						
All	*26.9*	*10.8*	*37.9*	*26.8*	*46.8*	*17.6*
Male	42.0	18.2	47.2	38.2	63.5	30.8
Female	0.7	2.1	27.1	15.8	3.5	2.5
Rural	32.2	—	51.4	—	50.5	—
Urban	17.3	—	27.5	—	37.4	—
25–59 years						
All	*49.7*	*60.7*	*62.8*	*57.8*	*69.0*	*53.7*
Male	96.2	97.2	98.0	93.2	97.6	96.2
Female	5.0	6.5	25.7	22.2	2.7	8.3
Rural	55.2	—	76.1	—	72.6	—
Urban	39.3	—	48.5	—	57.6	—
60 + years						
All	*14.8*	*26.4*	*10.9*	*11.2*	*30.6*	*20.6*
Male	32.0	43.0	23.1	19.5	52.4	36.6
Female	0.0	4.2	0.0	3.2	0.0	2.1
Rural	13.5	—	13.3	—	38.9	—
Urban	17.6	—	9.5	—	8.3	—
All ages						
All	*43.6*	*33.8*	*53.9*	*40.2*	*62.0*	*35.3*
Male	79.5	56.5	81.5	63.2	87.3	62.7
Female	4.2	4.0	24.6	17.5	2.3	5.3
Rural	49.0	—	62.6	—	66.1	—
Urban	33.2	—	39.5	—	48.7	—

may be explained partly in terms of the high proportion of workers in self-employment, i.e. about 23 and 27 per cent for in-migrants and non-migrants respectively.

It seems that female migrants in Uttar Pradesh do not migrate for employment and income reasons as much as in the other two states. That is why the proportion of female in-migrants is about 30 per cent in Uttar Pradesh while in Bihar and Kerala it is about 48 per cent, as noted in Section 3. It should be noted that the proportion of Muslims among the in-migrants was highest in Uttar Pradesh, and that the

Table 7.2: Female labour force paticipation rates by age, migration status and religion and caste group

State/age migration status	Religion and caste group			
	Hindus (other than Scheduled Castes)	Scheduled Castes/ Tribes	Muslims	Christians
Bihar				
All	2.7	10.3	3.0	33.3
Age (Years)				
10–19	0.5	4.1	0.7	28.6(*)
20–29	3.7	9.7	5.0	0.0(*)
30–59	4.5	15.0	3.1	42.9
60+	0.0	8.7	9.5	—
Migration status				
In-migrant	2.3	11.8	3.1	33.3(*)
Non-migrant	4.0	5.0	2.3	33.3(*)
Kerala				
All	21.5	25.7	7.7	18.3
Age (years)				
10–19	10.8	8.6	5.0	6.9
20–29	38.7	43.5	12.2	30.9
30–59	22.5	33.3	8.4	21.0
60+	2.5	0.0(*)	2.5	4.1
Migration status				
In-migrant	20.7	24.0	7.4	17.4
Non-migrant	25.3	60.0(*)	13.3	23.6
Uttar Pradesh				
All	4.5	13.4	2.2	21.0
Age (years)				
10–19	1.4	1.5	0.0	0.0(*)
20–29	4.5	11.9	2.7	28.6(*)
30–59	7.2	22.3	4.3	18.2
60+	1.2	14.3	0.0(*)	0.0(*)
Migration status				
In-migrant	4.8	14.2	2.1	26.7(*)
Non-migrant	2.2	8.6	2.8	0.0(*)

(*) Based on less than 10 observations.

Muslim religion discourages women from working. This is also reflected in the data related to female labour force participation rates by religion and caste groups given in table 7.2.

The data also suggest that female participation rates are generally higher among Christians and Scheduled Castes/Tribes than among other categories. This difference persists within each age group. The regression results presented in tables 7.3–7.5 overall confirm the findings discussed above. In Bihar, for example, among males in the 10–24 age group, in-migrants have a higher participation rate than non-migrants. Married males, because of their greater need for income, show higher participation rates (also true of the 25–59 age group). The participation rate is also higher if the household owns an enterprise, probably because it can make use of young family members as workers. The negative association with per capita income suggests that those in the higher income brackets prefer that their children be educated rather than work. In the 25–59 age group, in-migrants are at a disadvantage because of their late entry into the labour market, a disadvantage which is not suffered by the younger age group (10–24 years). In the case of married females and males in the 60+ age group, there is a negative association between per capita income and participation rate, suggesting that in the higher income brackets married females and older males prefer not to work. Among the females, whether married or unmarried, participation rates are higher for Scheduled Castes/Tribes and increase as a function of age.

The picture is not very different in Uttar Pradesh except that among in-migrants the differences in the participation rates between the 10–24 and 25–59 age groups is not so pronounced as in Bihar. Higher per capita income here too leads to lower participation rates among males of all age groups, but not among females. Among the Scheduled Castes/Tribes married females show higher participation rates, but for both married and unmarried females the participation rate increases with age, as was found in Bihar.

In Kerala, on the other hand, for males of all age groups and females whether married or unmarried, the results show that participation rates decrease as a function of per capita income. Married women from Scheduled Castes/Tribes show a higher participation rate, as in Uttar Pradesh. However, Muslim women in Kerala shun work. So far as age is concerned, the participation rate increases as a function of age only for unmarried women, maybe because with respect to migration status, among the unmarried, in-migrants have a higher participation rate than non-migrants, whereas in the case of married people, the natives show a higher participation rate.

Table 7.3: Estimated regression equations for the determinants of male and female labour participation rates in Bihar (t-values are given in brackets)

Variables		Males			Females	
		10–24 yrs.	25–59 yrs.	60 + yrs.	Married	Unmarried
HEAD	1 if head of household, 0 otherwise	—	0.045** (4.29) -	0.343** (4.43)	—	—
MRRD	1 if married, 0 otherwise	0.267** (9.79)	0.096** (6.64)	0.077 (0.96)	—	—
EDN1	1 if has no formal education, 0 otherwise	—	—	—	—	—
EDN2	1 if has less than secondary education, 0 otherwise	0.105** (5.86)	0.039** (3.37)	0.066 (0.90)	−0.004 (0.40)	−0.061** (4.29)
EDN3	1 if has secondary education, 0 otherwise	—	0.032** (2.65)	0.209* (2.02)	0.077** (5.47)	−0.065** (3.88)
EDN4	1 if a graduate or above, 0 otherwise	—	0.015 (1.18)	0.277 (1.48)	0.262* (11.79)	0.060* (2.19)
NNMG	1 if non-migrant, 0 otherwise	—	—	—	—	—
INMG	1 if in-migrant, 0 otherwise	0.044 + (1.83)	—	0.006 (0.06)	—	0.001 (0.07)
YSM1	1 if years since in-migration 0–4, 0 otherwise	—	−0.038** (2.14)	—	−0.012 (0.76)	—
YSM2	1 if years since in-migration 5–9, 0 otherwise	—	−0.022 + (1.73)	—	−0.022 + (1.65)	—

Variable	Description					
YSM3	1 if years since in-migration 10+, 0 otherwise	—	-0.020** (2.00)	—	0.007 (0.53)	0.003** (3.91)
AGE	Age (years)	-0.043** (2.73)	0.027** (6.69)	-0.165** (2.94)	0.001** (2.51)	—
AGES	Square of age	0.003** (5.50)	-36.527** (7.32)	0.001** (2.73)	—	—
RAC1	1 if Hindu/Christian, 0 otherwise	—	—	—	—	—
RAC2	1 if Scheduled Caste/ Tribe, 0 otherwise	—	—	—	0.064** (4.96)	0.060** (3.74)
RAC3	1 if Muslim, 0 otherwise	—	—	—	-0.006 (0.44)	0.004 (0.29)
ENTR	1 if household owns an enterprise 0 otherwise	0.152** (7.98)	0.013 (1.33)	0.032 (0.45)	—	—
PFIX	Per capita family income, excluding income of respondent	-0.559** (2.54)	-0.179 (1.58)	-4.734** (2.75)	-0.050** (4.25)	-0.071 (0.66)
	Constant	0.075	0.351		-0.095	0.023
	R^2	0.357	0.096	0.272	0.086	0.078
	F	151.787	20.130	6.417	19.932	12.460
	(N)	(1 919)	(2 280)	(183)	(2 130)	(1 185)

** significant at 1 per cent level.
* significant at 5 per cent level.
+ significant at 10 per cent level.

Table 7.4: Estimated regression equations for the determinants of male and female labour participation rates in Kerala (t-values are given in brackets)

Variables		Males			Females	
		10–24 yrs.	25–59 yrs.	60 + yrs.	Married	Unmarried
HEAD	1 if head of household, 0 otherwise	—	0.009 (0.62)	0.048 (0.75)	—	—
MRRD	1 if married, 0 otherwise	−0.034 (0.46)	0.035** (2.35)	0.046 (0.79)	—	—
EDN1	1 if has no formal education, 0 otherwise	—	—	—	—	—
EDN2	1 if has less than secondary education. 0 otherwise	0.355** (14.88)	0.133*** (3.61)	−0.083 (1.05)	−0.018 (0.48)	−0.376** (3.97)
EDN3	1 if has secondary education, 0 otherwise	—	0.145** (3.86)	−0.152+ (1.68)	0.200** (4.73)	−0.334** (3.51)
EDN4	1 if a graduate or above, 0 otherwise	—	0.167** (4.42)	0.069 (0.62)	0.538** (11.37)	−0.035 (0.34)
NNMG	1 if non-migrant, 0 otherwise	—	—	—	—	—
INMG	1 if in-migrant, 0 otherwise	0.019 (0.59)	—	0.052 (0.68)	—	0.184** (4.74)
YSM1	1 if years since in-migration 0–4 0 otherwise	—	−0.026 (1.24)	—	−0.084** (2.79)	—
YSM2	1 if years since in-migration 5–9, 0 otherwise	—	−0.006 (0.27)	—	−0.076 (2.22)	—
YSM3	1 if years since in-migration 10 +, 0 otherwise	—	0.015 (0.66)	—	0.014 (0.30)	—

Variable	Description	(1)	(2)	(3)	(4)	(5)
AGE	Age (years)	0.059** (2.85)	0.045** (8.24)	-0.089** (1.98)	81.146 (1.15)	0.020** (12.74)
AGES	Square of age	74.297 (1.25)	-64.169** (9.86)	0.001+ (1.73)	—	—
RAC1	1 if Hindu/Christian, 0 otherwise	—	—	—	—	—
RAC2	1 if Scheduled Caste/Tribe, 0 otherwise	—	—	—	0.107* (2.05)	0.016 (0.30)
RAC3	1 if Muslim, 0 otherwise	—	—	—	-0.061** (2.56)	-0.118** (4.21)
ENTR	1 if household owns an enterprise, 0 otherwise	-0.006 (0.27)	0.068** (5.09)	0.321** (5.91)	—	—
PFIX	Per capita family income, excluding income of respondent	-2.272** (5.61)	-1.816** (7.86)	-1.547** (2.37)	-2.429** (8.52)	-1.841** (4.52)
	Constant	-1.027	0.067		0.198	0.274
	R²	0.513	0.204	0.202	0.215	0.259
	F	192.026	37.450	8.172	48.534	53.598
	(N)	(1 285)	(1 770)	(333)	(1 778)	(1 236)

** significant at 1 per cent level.
* significant at 5 per cent level.
+ Significant at 10 per cent level.

Table 7.5: Estimated regression equations for the determinants of male and female labour participation rates in Uttar Pradesh (t-values are given in brackets)

Variables		Males			Females	
		10–24 yrs.	25–59 yrs.	60 + yrs.	Married	Unmarried
HEAD	1 if head of household, 0 otherwise	—	0.007 (0.65)	0.394** (4.94)	—	—
MRRD	1 if married, 0 otherwise	0.186** (6.10)	0.096** (7.67)	−0.107 (1.52)	—	—
EDN1	1 if has no formal education, 0 otherwise	—	—	—	—	—
EDN2	1 if has less than secondary education, 0 otherwise	0.187** (8.12)	0.018 (1.43)	0.061 (0.88)	−0.012 (1.17)	−0.014 (0.66)
EDN3	1 if has secondary education, 0 otherwise	—	0.026* (2.14)	−0.124 (1.57)	0.001 (0.11)	−0.043 + (1.93)
EDN4	1 if a graduate or above, 0 otherwise	—	0.019 (1.45)	−0.007 (0.06)	0.092** (5.92)	0.045 + (1.65)
NNMG	1 if non-migrant, 0 otherwise	—	—	—	—	—
INMG	1 if in-migrant, 0 otherwise	−0.009 (0.32)	—	0.156 (1.57)	—	0.004 (0.12)
YSM1	1 if years since in-migration 0–4, 0 otherwise	—	−0.009 (0.53)	—	−0.027 (1.47)	—
YSM2	1 if years since in-migration 5–9, 0 otherwise	—	−0.035** (2.67)	—	−0.027 (1.57)	—

		(1)	(2)	(3)	(4)	(5)
YSM3	1 if years since in-migration 10 +, 0 otherwise	—	-11.065 (0.01)	—	0.013 (0.61)	—
AGE	Age (years)	0.050** (2.73)	0.018** (4.57)	0.097 + (1.89)	83.030** (2.33)	0.010** (6.81)
AGES	Square of age	63.527 (1.17)	-27.762** (5.59)	56.956 (1.60)	—	—
RAC1	1 if Hindu/Christian, 0 otherwise	—	—	—	—	—
RAC2	1 if Scheduled Caste/Tribe, 0 otherwise	—	—	—	0.087** (5.69)	0.002 (0.09)
RAC3	1 if Muslim, 0 otherwise	—	—	—	-0.003 (0.17)	-9.019 (0.89)
ENTR	1 if household owns an enterprise, 0 otherwise	0.051** (2.46)	-0.006 (0.66)	0.106 + (1.76)	—	—
PFIX	Per capita family income, excluding income of respondent	-3.029** (7.03)	-0.633** (3.89)	-6.178** (4.03)	-0.181 (1.16)	-0.323 (0.88)
	Constant	-0.722	7.987	4.145	30.200	-0.092
	R^2	0.471	0.092	0.291	0.045	0.113
	F	209.237	17.892	9.266	14.503	—
	(N)	(1656)	(2129)	(242)	(1972)	(917)

** significant at 1 per cent level.

* significant at 5 per cent level.

+ Significant at 10 per cent level.

CHAPTER 8

MIGRATION AND THE STRUCTURE OF THE URBAN LABOUR MARKET

A first approximation about the role of migrant workers in an urban economy can be made by examining the relative distribution of in-migrant and non-migrant workers among different occupations (Banerjee, 1986). In Bihar, though there is not much difference between in-migrants and non-migrants so far as occupational distribution is concerned, it can be said that the in-migrants' share in the professional/administrative occupations is a little larger than that of non-migrants (table 8.1). It is also evident that among in-migrants, this share is relatively larger for those with a longer duration of stay than for more recent ones. The recent migrants' share in clerical and sales occupations is distinctly larger than that of the earlier migrants. Other differences are marginal except that the proportion of wage/ salary earners is higher and the proportion of self-employed correspondingly lower among in-migrants than among non-migrants; among in-migrants, there is a clear tendency to shift from wage employment to self-employment over time (table 8.2). Though, on average, there is no difference between the proportion of workers in public sector employment among in-migrants and non-migrants, there are significant differences within different categories of in-migrants. The share of public sector employment in total employment is smaller among recent in-migrants (0–4 years' standing) as compared with in-migrants of 5–9 years' and more than 10 years' standing. This may suggest that either the growth in public sector employment has been lagging behind the growth of the labour force or many in-migrants initially join the private sector and then slowly move into public sector employment, which offers greater job security. It must be noted that the public sector accounts for about two-thirds of total employment in urban Bihar, whereas both in Kerala and in Uttar Pradesh the figure is less than half.

In Uttar Pradesh, the shares of service and production related work are higher for in-migrants than non-migrants, with recent in-migrants having a larger share of service work than earlier ones (table 8.1). As far as employment status is concerned, in Uttar Pradesh, too, wage earning is more prevalent among in-migrants than non-migrants; but, unlike in Bihar, here the in-migrants' shift from wage employment to self-employment is véry limited (table 8.2). Although in-migrants have a smaller share of public sector jobs than non-migrants, there is a significant improvement in this share over time.

As regards occupational structure, Kerala's situation is similar to that of Bihar except that in-migrants in Kerala have a larger share of service and clerical work than non-migrants (table 8.1). It is also interesting to note that a relatively làrge proportion of workers in Kerala, both in-migrants and non-migrants, are in clerical occupations, whereas in Bihar and Uttar Pradesh the largest proportions of workers are engaged in production and service related activities respectively. In Kerala, there is hardly any difference between in-migrants and non-migrants so far as the share of wage employment is concerned (table 8.2). But, unlike in Uttar Pradesh, the in-migrants' share in public sector jobs in Kerala is larger than that of non-migrants.

Some interesting differences in the structure of employment can also be observed between in-migrants from urban areas and those migrating from rural areas. This is because in-migrants from urban areas are likely to be'more skilled and experienced than those from rural areas. In Bihar, while in-migrants from urban areas have a larger share in occupations like professional/administrative, clerical and sales work, those migrating from rural areas have a larger share in production related occupations (table 8.1). There is hardly any perceptible difference with respect to the share of wage employment and public sector employment (table 8.2). The situation with regard to occupational structure is similar in Uttar Pradesh, except that the share of in-migrants from rural areas in service occupations is relatively more than that of in-migrants from urban areas (table 8.1). Whereas in Bihar there is no significant difference between in-migrants from rural and urban areas with respect to share of wage and public sector employment, in Uttar Pradesh the share of wage employment is relatively larger and of public sector employment relatively smaller among in-migrants from rural areas (table 8.2).

In Kerala, there are no significant differences in the occupational

Table 8.1: Percentage distribution of employed persons by occupation and migration status

State/occupation	In-migrants						Non-migrants
	Years since migration			Previous place of residence		All	
	0–4	5–9	10 +	Rural	Urban		
Bihar							
(N)	(136)	(240)	(371)	(531)	(216)	(747)	(2 638)
Professional/ administrative	18.1	16.9	25.2	19.0	30.4	21.9	15.9
Clerical	22.6	15.5	12.5	13.6	18.9	15.3	17.7
Sales	19.5	15.5	15.7	13.7	23.4	16.4	18.9
Service	11.3	11.8	9.2	10.7	10.0	10.0	12.0
Production-related	26.3	31.9	30.9	35.0	17.4	30.4	32.0
Others	2.3	6.3	6.3	8.0	0.0	5.6	3.5
Kerala							
(N)	(187)	(154)	(132)	(288)	(185)	(473)	(2 263)
Professional/ administrative	14.3	23.2	22.6	18.8	21.1	19.6	17.9
Clerical	28.2	29.1	27.3	29.2	26.9	28.3	23.6
Sales	9.4	9.3	7.8	9.0	8.8	8.9	11.6
Service	16.6	10.6	6.3	13.5	8.8	11.7	8.0
Production-related	8.8	8.6	9.4	8.0	10.5	8.9	11.4
Others	22.7	19.2	26.7	21.5	24.0	22.6	27.4

Uttar Pradesh

(N)	(168)	(277)	(241)	(490)	(196)	(686)	(1 823)
Professional/administrative	7.0	5.9	5.2	3.9	12.2	5.9	14.9
Clerical	12.2	17.9	13.9	13.1	21.3	15.2	19.0
Sales	22.4	14.6	18.7	16.7	21.3	17.5	22.2
Service	34.0	30.6	25.2	30.8	25.6	29.4	23.2
Production-related	22.4	25.7	35.7	32.0	17.7	29.0	19.3
Others	1.9	5.2	1.3	3.2	1.8	2.9	1.5

Table 8.2: Percentage of workers in wage employment; public sector employment and formal sector employment among in-migrants and non-migrants

State/occupation	In-migrants						Non-migrants
	Years since migration			Previous place of residence		All	
	0–4	5–9	10 +	Rural	Urban		
Percentage of workers in wage employment							
Bihar	85.7	75.9	72.0	76.2	74.0	75.7	72.9
Kerala	88.4	84.1	83.3	87.1	88.9	85.6	85.5
Uttar Pradesh	79.5	88.0	81.3	84.9	71.8	83.9	78.9
Percentage of workers in Public sector							
Bihar	58.2	61.9	68.1	63.9	64.0	64.2	63.2
Kerala	52.4	58.8	52.5	48.3	65.4	54.4	42.2
Uttar Pradesh	24.0	28.6	36.0	29.7	37.2	31.3	45.6
Percentage of workers in formal sector							
Bihar	65.9	67.9	73.9	65.9	81.8	70.5	70.3
Kerala	60.0	72.2	75.4	62.5	78.2	68.2	58.6
Uttar Pradesh	38.4	45.4	55.3	40.5	66.1	47.5	63.4

distributions of in-migrants coming from rural and urban areas, unlike in Bihar and Uttar Pradesh where a relatively lower proportion of in-migrants from rural areas are engaged in white-collar jobs, as noted above (table 8.1). This implies that differentials in skill and experience between in-migrants from rural and urban areas are more pronounced in Bihar and Uttar Pradesh than in Kerala, where the overall level of education is higher.

There is no significant difference between the proportion of workers in the formal sector among in-migrants and non-migrants in Bihar; the proportion is higher for non-migrants in Uttar Pradesh and for in-migrants in Kerala (table 8.2). The data also show that a relatively large proportion of in-migrants get absorbed in the formal sector in Bihar and Kerala as compared to Uttar Pradesh. In all three states, the absorption of in-migrants in the formal sector increases as a function of their duration of stay in the city. This is true for in-migrants both from rural and urban areas (table 8.3).

Here again, the difference in the share of formal sector employment between in-migrants from rural and urban areas is more important than that between in-migrants and non-migrants. It will be seen that in all three states, in-migrants from urban areas have a relatively larger share of formal sector employment. This may imply that there is a greater selectivity with respect to education and skills among urban-urban migrants than among rural-urban migrants.

So far as employment status is concerned, the share of the formal sector in self-employment is lower in Bihar and Uttar Pradesh than in Kerala. This may imply that infrastructure facilities such as credit and training are more organized in Kerala than in the other two states. The relatively higher level of education in Kerala and the higher quantum of remittances from migrants to Gulf countries may also be relevant here. In the case of wage employment, the share of the formal sector in Uttar Pradesh is much lower than in Bihar and Kerala. This may be due to the greater skill requirements in public sector employment in Bihar because of the Bokaro Steel Industry and in Kerala because of higher levels of education.

With respect to education, the majority of those with secondary education or above get absorbed in the formal sector. Among those who have some formal education, although a lower proportion enter the formal sector to begin with, they gradually improve their position. This improvement is more marked in Bihar and Uttar Pradesh than in Kerala.

Table 8.3: Percentage of workers in the formal sector among in-migrants and non-migrants for different categories of workers

States/categories	In-migrants				Non-migrants
	Years since migration			All	
	0–4	5–9	10+		
Bihar					
Employment status					
Self-employed	39.9	43.6	59.2	52.1	65.7
Wage/salary earner	69.6	77.3	80.8	77.4	74.3
Education					
No formal education	23.1	31.8	28.9	28.7	33.2
Less than secondary	39.1	50.0	62.3	54.4	62.7
Secondary	87.8	84.4	91.7	88.3	89.3
Graduate and above	93.8	93.5	100.0	96.9	96.8
Previous place of residence					
Rural	60.0	63.2	69.5	65.9	—
Urban	80.0	77.1	86.0	81.8	—
Kerala					
Employment status					
Self-employed	76.5	77.8	78.6	77.6	63.8
Wage/salary earner	62.0	73.0	75.2	69.2	59.6
Education					
No formal educaton	—	—	—	10.0	16.4
Less than secondary	23.3	39.1	25.7	28.6	30.9
Secondary	77.4	81.4	91.2	83.4	83.1
Graduate and above	94.9	100.0	100.0	97.8	95.2
Previous place of residence					
Rural	52.1	69.1	69.9	62.5	—
Urban	73.2	77.2	87.0	78.2	—
Uttar Pradesh					
Employment status					
Self-employed	48.0	62.1	64.1	59.1	64.7
Wage/salary earner	40.5	45.0	56.8	48.0	70.3
Education					
No formal education	4.8	29.0	42.1	30.7	37.8
Less than secondary	21.7	20.8	44.9	30.0	49.6
Secondary	47.3	47.1	59.7	51.2	68.6
Graduate and above	79.3	90.9	88.8	87.5	88.5
Previous place of residence					
Rural	28.0	38.3	50.5	40.5	—
Urban	63.8	63.0	72.9	66.1	—

The regression results presented in table 8.4 by and large confirm the above findings. However, certain aspects come into sharper focus. With respect to migration status, in Bihar, in-migrants from the rural areas have a relative disadvantage as regards getting absorbed in the formal sector as self-employed workers. However, in-migrants from urban areas, though initially at a disadvantage, gradually improve their position. In Uttar Pradesh, too, in-migrants from the rural areas suffer some initial disadvantage as regards self-employment in the formal sector but it disappears eventually. It is also interesting to note that even with respect to wage employment in Uttar Pradesh, in-migrants from the rural areas are always at a disadvantage so far as absorption in the formal sector is concerned. It seems that urban labour markets in Uttar Pradesh have relatively low labour mobility compared to those in the other two states.

In addition, the regression results show that Muslims are at a relative disadvantage as regards wage employment in the formal sector in all three states, and Scheduled Castes/Tribes in Kerala. In Bihar, however, Muslims and Scheduled Castes/Tribes have a positive advantage as regards self-employment in the formal sector.

Unemployment is another important feature of urban labour markets. About 6 per cent of the labour force reported unemployment in Bihar, 8 per cent in Uttar Pradesh and 21 per cent in Kerala[1] (table 8.5). It is also interesting to note that though unemployment is concentrated among the secondary household workers (i.e. sons/ daughters and other relatives), in Kerala there is considerable unemployment even among the heads of households. It is also evident from the table that in all three states unemployment is more acute among non-migrants than in-migrants, and among the educated than among those with no formal education. Though the percentage of the labour force that is unemployed is lowest in Bihar, the figure for those who remain unemployed for more than three years is as high as 42 per cent (table 8.6). As regards those remaining unemployed for more than a year, the figures are about 78 per cent in Bihar, 56 per cent in Uttar Pradesh and 34 per cent in Kerala. It is this long duration of unemployment which causes lumpenisation and criminalisation in the urban centres. The data also show that there is a long waiting period not only among first time job-seekers but also among those

---

[1] The labour force consists of employed and unemployed persons. A person was considered unemployed if he/she was not gainfully employed even for one hour during the referene period (i.e. 7 days preceding the date of the survey).

Table 8.4: Estimated regression equations for the determinants of employment in the formal sector (t-values are given in brackets)

Variable	Bihar		Kerala		Uttar Pradesh	
	Self-employed	Wage/salary earner	Self-employed	Wage/salary earner	Self-employed	Wage/salary earner
AGE Age (years)	22.229 (0.16)	0.007** (8.68)	0.005* (2.17)	0.007** (8.73)	0.003 (1.58)	0.008** (9.37)
MALE 1 if male, 0 otherwise	0.187 (1.36)	-0.027 (0.79)	-0.141 (1.06)	-0.014 (0.67)	0.185+ (1.70)	0.029 (0.73)
EDN1 1 if no formal education, 0 otherwise	—	—	—	—	—	—
EDN2 1 if less than secondary, 0 otherwise	0.092+ (1.78)	0.347** (13.52)	0.217 (1.42)	0.193** (3.76)	0.153+ (1.92)	0.0666* (2.26)
EDN3 1 if secondary education, 0 otherwise	0.298** (4.76)	0.633** (23.61)	0.523** (3.21)	0.758** (14.54)	0.192* (2.29)	0.295** (9.82)
EDN4 1 if graduate or above, 0 otherwise	0.420** (5.15)	0.682** (23.66)	0.440** (2.61)	0.887** (16.93)	0.400** (4.09)	0.527** (16.57)
RAC1 1 if Hindu/Christian, 0 otherwise	—	—	—	—	—	—
RAC2 1 if Scheduled Caste/Tribe, 0 otherwise	0.183** (2.82)	-0.010 (0.41)	0.060 (0.31)	-0.112** (2.62)	0.029 (0.27)	0.016 (0.51)
RAC3 1 if Muslim, 0 otherwise	0.157** (3.27)	-0.180** (6.64)	0.003 (0.04)	-0.078** (2.93)	0.075 (0.90)	-0.215 (6.08)
NNMG 1 if non-migrant, 0 otherwise						
RYM1 1 if in-migrated from rural areas in last						

		(1)	(2)	(3)	(4)	(5)	(6)
RYM2	0–4 years, 0 otherwise 1 if in-migrated from rural areas in last	−0.235** (5.00)	−0.219+ (1.98)	−0.012 (0.33)	0.166 (1.04)	−0.063 (1.63)	−0.270+ (1.92)
	5–9 years, 0 otherwise	−0.176** (5.18)	0.046 (0.41)	0.010 (0.25)	0.169 (1.29)	0.035 (1.10)	−0.437** (5.27)
RYM3	1 if in-migrated from rural areas 10 + years ago, 0 otherwise	−0.074* (2.13)	−0.071 (0.73)	−0.032 (0.76)	0.008 (0.04)	0.029 (1.11)	−0.117** (2.11)
UYM1	1 if in-migrated from urban areas in last 0–4 years/ 0 otherwise	−0.028 (0.40)	0.139 (0.65)	−2.521 (0.00)	−0.036 (0.22)	0.048 (0.71)	−0.340* (1.93)
UYM2	1 if in-migrated from urban areas in last 5–9 years, 0 otherwise	−0.025 (0.47)	−0.125 (0.82)	0.091 + (1.84)	−0.101 (0.49)	0.023 (0.44)	0.028 (0.28)
UYM3	1 if in-migrated from urban areas 10 + years ago, 0 otherwise	0.098 (1.33)	0.163 (1.22)	0.054 (0.89)	0.193 (1.17)	0.029 (0.69)	0.249** (2.34)
	Constant		0.157	−0.126	0.266	0.075	0.276
	R^2	0.132	0.085	0.503	0.136	0.392	0.128
	F	62.351	2.717	145.178	2.759	94.086	7.385
	(N)	(1 985)	(395)	(1 881)	(241)	(1 913)	(669)

** significant at 1 per cent level.
* significant at 5 per cent level.
+ significant at 10 per cent level.

Table 8.5: Percentage of the labour force who are unemployed by age, sex, relation to household head, education and migration status

	Bihar		Kerala		Uttar Pradesh	
	In-migrants	Non-migrants	In-migrants	Non-migrants	In-migrants	Non-migrants
All	5.3	6.3	7.7	23.8	4.2	9.4
Age (years)						
10–19	20.0	18.0	14.7	61.2	22.7	42.9
20–29	12.8	20.0	16.1	40.3	5.8	17.7
30–59	1.0	1.1	2.6	6.8	1.8	1.6
Sex						
Male	5.4	6.1	5.9	19.8	4.2	9.5
Female	2.8	9.4	14.0	38.2	0.0	8.4
Relation to head						
Head	0.8	0.5	3.2	5.3	0.9	0.9
Son/daughter	27.3	20.5	45.2	40.9	8.9	21.0
Others	16.9	11.8	8.6	23.5	16.2	14.5
Education						
No formal education	0.0	4.0	0.0	5.2	1.3	11.1
Less than secondary	6.0	4.8	7.0	25.4	4.7	9.2
Secondary	6.1	6.9	9.3	29.6	4.8	10.0
Graduate and above	5.8	10.8	6.8	15.1	5.5	7.7

who have worked before and are now seeking jobs. This is most pronounced in Bihar. With regard to migration status, in-migrants in Bihar have to wait relatively longer than both in-migrants and non-migrants in the other two states. Whereas in Uttar Pradesh, there is no difference between the proportion of in-migrants and non-migrants who remain unemployed for more than three years in Kerala, a relatively larger proportion of non-migrants do so.

Information about the job aspirations of the unemployed is presented in table 8.7. By and large more than 90 per cent aspire to wage employment, irrespective of their level of education. Among those with education levels less than graduate, both in Kerala and in Uttar Pradesh, a large proportion is prepared to work for less than Rs 500 a month, and the figure is higher among in-migrants. In Bihar this proportion is generally low, and is lower in the case of in-migrants. Among graduates, in Kerala more than three-quarters are prepared to work for less than Rs 500 a month. In Bihar and Uttar Pradesh this

Table 8.6: **Percentage distribution of unemployed persons by duration of unemployment**

State/ characteristics	Duration of unemployment				
	1–6 months	*7–12 months*	*1–3 years*	*3 + years*	*All*
Bihar					
All (N = 165)	9.7	12.1	36.4	41.8	100.0
Whether seeking job for first time					
Yes	12.1	15.0	36.4	36.4	100.0
No	5.4	7.1	33.9	52.6	100.0
Migration status					
In-migrant	7.1	9.5	31.0	52.4	100.0
Non-migrant	10.6	13.0	38.2	38.2	100.0
Kerala					
All (N = 492)	43.9	22.2	25.0	8.9	100.0
Whether seeking job for first time					
Yes	53.2	20.4	18.9	7.6	100.0
No	33.1	24.2	32.2	10.6	100.0
Migration status					
In-migrant	64.5	12.9	19.4	3.2	100.0
Non-migrant	42.5	22.8	25.4	9.4	100.0
Uttar Pradesh					
All (N = 228)	—	43.9	33.8	22.4	100.0
Whether seeking job for first time					
Yes	—	50.6	31.4	17.9	100.0
No	—	28.2	39.4	32.4	100.0
Migration status					
In-migrant	—	48.6	28.6	22.9	100.0
Non-migrant	—	43.0	34.7	22.3	100.0

Note: For Uttar Pradesh, the percentages for 7–12 months refer to the joint percentage for the first two duration groups.

proportion is much lower, particularly among non-migrants. All this clearly indicates that unemployment in these urban centres is not necessarily caused by high income expectations, particularly in the case of Kerala. It rather implies that urban labour markets are to some extent saturated.

In Kerala and Uttar Pradesh, those with educational levels of graduate and above are mostly looking for white-collar jobs, 100 per cent among in-migrants, even though their income expectations are

Table 8.7: Job aspirations of the unemployed by migration status and level of education

Level of education/ aspiration	Bihar		Kerala		Uttar Pradesh	
	In-migrants	Non-migrants	In-migrants	Non-migrants	In-migrants	Non-migrants
Less than graduate						
Percentage of unemployed looking for						
Professional/admin. job	6.2	6.9	10.5	1.2	9.1	3.5
clerical job	21.9	14.9	52.6	42.5	13.6	31.2
other jobs	71.9	78.2	36.9	49.3	77.3	65.2
Percentage of unemployed looking for wage employment	93.8	95.2	91.7	97.9	100.0	97.2
Percentage of unemployment prepared to work for less than Rs 500 a month	21.9	36.9	100.0	63.8	90.0	83.4
Graduate and above						
Percentage of unemployed looking for						
Professional/admin. job	20.0	18.4	22.2	6.2	8.3	17.0
clerical job	40.0	39.5	77.8	75.0	91.7	78.7
other jobs	40.0	42.0	0.0	18.8	0.0	4.3
Percentage of unemployed looking for wage employment	80.0	97.3	85.7	98.0	100.0	97.9
Percentage of unemployed prepared to work for less than Rs 500 a month	35.1	22.2	75.0	81.4	61.5	29.8

not high. In Bihar, only about 60 per cent of the graduate unemployed are looking for white-collar jobs. The data in general show, therefore, that there is an excess supply of labour for white-collar jobs, especially clerical jobs.

CHAPTER 9

MIGRATION AND THE STRUCTURE OF URBAN EARNINGS

Employment and income are the two important aspects, analysis of which leads to an understanding of the process of integration of in-migrants in the existing urban setting and of the contribution they are making to the urban economy and, through human and capital flows, to the rural economy. Analysis of employment and related data indicates that since urban centres do not appear to suffer from a shortage of labour, in-migration may have caused an excess supply of labour and might therefore have led, to some extent, to the process of criminalisation and lumpenisation of urban society.

In Uttar Pradesh, the average monthly income of employed persons is higher for non-migrants than for in-migrants, within all age groups and regardless of employment status (table 9.1). Overall, the average income of non-migrants is about 26 per cent higher. This may be for two reasons. First, non-migrants may possess greater skills and experience than in-migrants. Second, due to their longer association with an old industrial city like Kanpur, non-migrants may represent a superior workforce. The situation is just the opposite in Kerala, where in-migrants appear to have higher average incomes than non-migrants. There is no noteworthy difference between the mean income of in-migrants and non-migrants in Bihar. It is interesting to note, however, that earnings in public sector employment are somewhat higher among non-migrants than among in-migrants in all three states.

With respect to education, in both Bihar and Uttar Pradesh, among those with no formal education, in-migrants have a higher income than non-migrants. Otherwise, incomes are relatively higher for non-migrants. In Kerala, for graduates and above and for those with no formal education, the incomes of non-migrants are higher than those of in-migrants.

In all three states, as is evident from table 9.2, the average income of migrants from urban areas is higher than that of migrants from rural areas. This difference is particularly marked in the case of Uttar Pradesh, where the income of urban-urban in-migrants is on average 60 per cent higher than that of rural-urban in-migrants. In the other two states, this difference ranges between 20 and 25 per cent.

With increasing duration of stay, in-migrants in general show an improvement in their average income. A comparison of the average income of recent in-migrants (0–4 years) with that of long-standing in-migrants (10 + years) shows that in Bihar and Kerala, the increase in income is roughly 40 per cent, while in Uttar Pradesh it is only about 14 per cent (table 9.2). Whereas in Bihar and Kerala, rural-urban migrants show a higher rate of improvement in their average earning than urban-urban migrants, in Uttar Pradesh urban-urban in-migrants show twice as much improvement as rural-urban in-migrants.

As far as education is concerned, around 60 per cent improvement in income is apparent over time among in-migrants with no formal education in Bihar and among in-migrants with less than secondary education in Kerala. The relatively greater improvement in the case of those with low levels of education may be partly due to the fact that they usually begin at low levels of income. In the case of Bihar it should be noted that even graduates are able to improve their income by more than 50 per cent, as their length of stay in the city increases. The corresponding figures for both Kerala and Uttar Pradesh are less than 15 per cent. In Uttar Pradesh, improvements are small, irrespective of the level of education.

The multiple regression results given in table 9.3 more or less corroborate the above findings. As expected, the heads of households have higher incomes than others. Level of income goes up with age, except for the self-employed in Bihar. It should be noted that age is a proxy for experience. The exception in the case of urban Bihar may be due to poor infrastructure support for the private sector. In almost all cases in the three states, the level of earnings increases as a function of educational level. In all three states, Scheduled Castes/ Tribes have lower incomes than others, as do Muslims in Bihar.

With regard to migration status, the average incomes of those coming from urban areas do not appear to differ from those of non-migrants. It is the in-migrants from rural areas who are at a disadvantage in Bihar and Uttar Pradesh, except for the self-employed in Bihar. Whereas in both Bihar and Uttar Pradesh, the incomes of wage earners tend to improve, reaching the level of non-migrant incomes after about 10 years, no such improvement can be seen in the case of the self-employed in Uttar Pradesh.

Table 9.1: Average monthly income of employed persons by migration status and demographic and socio-economic characteristics (in rupees)

	Bihar		Kerala		Uttar Pradesh	
	In-migrants	Non-migrants	In-migrants	Non-migrants	In-migrants	Non-migrants
(N)	(728)	(1 857)	(453)	(1 714)	(642)	(1 788)
All	889	908	942	873	640	808
Age (years)						
10–19	363	274	245	255	260	308
20–29	653	501	754	675	539	637
30–44	1 018	1 010	1 110	997	736	898
45 +	930	1 069	957	933	699	854
Education						
No formal education	556	471	330	421	483	453
Less than secondary	687	717	572	531	504	597
Secondary	895	1 054	994	897	628	827
Graduate and above	1 404	1 579	1 312	1 575	1 081	1 219
Employment status						
Self-employed	855	839	1 056	841	821	944
Wage/salary earner	899	923	903	858	593	785
Occupation						
Professional/administrative	1 357	1 506	1 258	1 473	1 334	1 426
Clerical	953	1 013	952	940	741	875
Sales	756	835	760	640	806	839

Service	551	681	342	582	501	538
Production related	683	679	958	557	497	553
Others	964	962	1 011	677	447	799
Type of job						
Private sector	557	554	706	572	598	612
Public sector	1 103	1 138	1 147	1 274	745	944

Table 9.2: Average monthly income of employed persons by education, migration status, years since migration and previous place of residence (in rupees)

States/education/ previous place of residence	In-migrants				Non-migrants
	Years since migration			All	
	0–4	5–9	10+		
Bihar					
All	720	767	1 011	889	908
Education					
No formal education	358	616	570	556	471
Less than secondary	584	603	767	687	717
Secondary	720	769	1 045	895	1 054
Graduate and above	1 073	1 160	1 642	1 404	1 579
Previous place of residence					
Rural	637	731	959	832	—
Urban	965	861	1 150	1 014	—
Kerala					
All	771	958	1 066	942	873
Education					
No formal education	—	—	—	330	421
Less than secondary	398	661	655	572	531
Secondary	843	929	1 131	994	897
Graduate and above	1 220	1 369	1 392	1 312	1 575
Previous place of residence					
Rural	632	941	1 010	836	—
Urban	1 009	986	1 185	1 048	—
Uttar Pradesh					
All	589	561	673	640	808
Education					
No formal education	430	422	526	483	453
Less than secondary	432	478	512	504	597
Secondary	569	507	699	628	827
Graduate and above	1 069	908	1 203	1 081	1 219
Previous place of residence					
Rural	516	478	586	527	—
Urban	772	789	1 014	849	—

Table 9.3: Estimated regression equations for the determinants of annual income of employed persons (Dependent variable: log of annual income) (t-values are given in brackets)

Variable		Bihar		Kerala		Uttar Pradesh	
		Self-employed	Wage/earners	Self-employed	Wage/earners	Self-employed	Wage/earners
HEAD	1 if head of household, 0 otherwise	0.174** (3.43)	0.043** (2.40)	−0.056 (0.90)	−0.050** (2.99)	0.031 (0.63)	0.071** (4.56)
SNDT	1 if son/daughter of head, 0 otherwise	0.115+ (1.94)	−0.008 (0.35)	−0.069 (1.06)	−0.002 (0.13)	0.020 (0.38)	0.005 (0.30)
OTHR	1 if other relation of head, 0 otherwise	—	—	—	—	—	—
AGE1	1 if age 10–19, 0 otherwise	—	—	—	—	—	—
AGE2	1 if age 20–29, 0 otherwise	−0.038 (0.42)	0.181** (6.22)	0.228+ (1.85)	0.173** (6.54)	0.211* (2.20)	0.164** (5.94)
AGE3	1 if age 30–39, 0 otherwise	0.038 (0.40)	0.219** (7.30)	0.288** (2.26)	0.135** (8.55)	0.304** (3.15)	0.237** (8.32)
AGE4	1 if age 40–49, 0 otherwise	0.099 (1.03)	0.271** (8.75)	0.377** (2.80)	0.268** (9.03)	0.268** (2.64)	0.282** (9.39)
AGE5	1 if age 50–59, 0 otherwise	0.086 (0.84)	0.277** (8.52)	0.309 (2.30)	0.254** (8.10)	0.296** (2.74)	0.306** (9.72)
AGE6	1 if age 60+, 0 otherwise	0.021 (0.21)	0.082+ (1.81)	0.446** (3.14)	0.192** (4.37)	.0.300** (2.77)	0.204** (5.40)
EDN1	1 if has no formal education, 0 otherwise						

Table 9.3: (*Contd.*)

Variable		Bihar		Kerala		Uttar Pradesh	
		Self-employed	Wage/earners	Self-employed	Wage/earners	Self-employed	Wage/earners
EDN2	1 if has less than secondary education, 0 otherwise	0.082* (1.96)	0.131** (8.40)	—	—	0.017 (0.36)	0.052** (3.62)
EDN3	1 if has secondary education, 0 otherwise	0.182** (3.45)	0.233** (13.33)	0.077+ (1.74)	0.205** (14.28)	0.163** (3.25)	0.131** (8.81)
EDN4	1 if a graduate or above	0.254** (3.84)	0.365** (19.36)	0.261** (5.00)	0.384** (24.47)	0.389** (6.76)	0.317** (19.80)
MALE	1 if male, 0 otherwise	0.294** (2.63)	0.148** (7.28)	0.345** (4.54)	0.161** (12.02)	0.192** (2.98)	0.277** (14.00)
RAC1	1 if a Hindu, 0 otherwise	—	—	—	—	—	—
RAC2	1 if a Scheduled Caste/Tribe, 0 otherwise	−0.336** (6.42)	−0.039** (2.82)	−0.288** (2.55)	−0.064* (2.25)	−0.210** (3.38)	−0.007 (0.48)
RAC3	1 if a Muslim, 0 otherwise	−0.204** (5.01)	−0.048** (2.99)	−0.042 (0.94)	0.020 (1.09)	−0.060 (1.25)	0.021 (1.21)
RAC4	1 if a Christian, 0 otherwise	—	—	0.063 (1.38)	0.041** (3.40)	—	—
NNMG	1 if a non-migrant 0 otherwise	—	—	—	—	—	—
RYM1	1 if in-migrated from rural areas in last 0–4 years, 0 otherwise	−0.103 (0.99)	−0.053* (2.30)	0.111 (1.13)	−0.014 (0.57)	−0.133* (2.03)	−0.071** (2.98)
RYM2	1 if in-migrated from rural areas in last 5–9 years, 0 otherwise	0.050 (0.69)	−0.042* (2.21)	0.131+ (1.68)	0.004 (0.15)	−0.050 (0.77)	−0.060** (3.42)

	1	2	3	4	5	6
RYM3 1 if in-migrated from rural areas 10+ years ago 0 otherwise	0.003 (0.07)	0.023 (1.43)	0.140 (1.23)	0.043 (1.56)	−0.113* (1.96)	−0.028 (1.59)
UYM1 1 if in-migrated from urban areas in last 0–4 years 0 otherwise	−0.094 (0.67)	0.021 (0.55)	0.117 (1.21)	0.006 (0.19)	−0.029 (0.24)	0.033 (0.96)
UYM2 1 if in-migrated from urban areas in last 5–9 years, 0 otherwise	−0.048 (0.59)	0.014 (0.46)	0.047 (0.39)	−0.010 (0.30)	−0.114 (1.27)	0.030 (1.14)
UYM3 1 if in-migrated from urban areas 10+ years ago 0 otherwise	0.130 (1.50)	0.049* (1.98)	0.137 (1.38)	0.041 (1.02)	0.114 (1.45)	−0.025 (0.68)
PSEC 1 if employed in public sector, 0 otherwise	—	0.263** (21.64)	—	0.200** (15.19)	—	0.135** (13.73)
Constant	3.430	3.182	3.260	3.252	3.349	3.123
R^2	0.256	0.630	0.300	0.598	0.329	0.490
F	9.150	159.159	4.945	138.034	9.665	94.483
(N)	(524)	(1 889)	(239)	(1 875)	(394)	(1 985)

** Significant at 1 per cent level.
 * Significant at 5 per cent level.
 + Significant at 10 per cent level.

CHAPTER 10

REMITTANCES BY URBAN IN-MIGRANTS AND THEIR EFFECT ON THE LEVEL AND DISTRIBUTION OF URBAN HOUSEHOLD INCOME

Taking rural and urban areas together, the percentage of employed in-migrants who remit money to their family, relations and friends back home is 22.8 in Bihar, 35.1 in Uttar Pradesh and 35.2 in Kerala (table 10.1). In all three states, the percentage of remitters is lower among in-migrants from urban areas than those from rural areas. This is because urban-urban migration is usually dominated more by family rather than individual migration compared to rural-urban migration. Moreover, the joint family system and property ties are normally weaker among in-migrants from urban areas. The proportion of remitters is highest, about 80 per cent, for the category of married heads living alone, probably because they have an obligation to provide for the needs of the family members who have stayed behind. The next highest proportion is among unmarried heads living alone. With respect to years since migration, in Bihar there is no noticeable decline in the proportion of remitters over time, whereas there is a marked decline in Kerala. Uttar Pradesh presents a mixed picture. While the proportion of remitters shows a decline over time in the case of urban-urban migrants, there is a distinct increase over time among rural-urban migrants.

So far as educational level is concerned, it was found that in Bihar the proportion of remitters declines sharply with increases in the level of education, for in-migrants from both rural and urban areas, so much so that the proportions among the graduate level and above are only 15 and 13 per cent respectively. In Kerala and Uttar Pradesh the pattern is mixed. However, it should be noted that in all three states the percentage of remitters is lower among those with graduate level education and above as compared to those with less than secondary level.

There tends to be a higher proportion of remitters among Scheduled Castes/Tribes than other groups in Kerala and Uttar Pradesh, but not in Bihar. This may be an indication of a higher level of poverty among employed Scheduled Castes/Tribes in Bihar.

It will be seen that the proportion of remitters is generally higher among wage earners than among the self-employed. With regard to land status in the previous place of residence, there is no perceptible difference in the proportion of remitters from landless and landed households in rural areas.

In Uttar Pradesh, the proportion of remitters from among the top 30 per cent of the household income category is larger than that among the bottom 30 per cent, irrespective of whether they came from rural or urban areas. The same is true for the remitters among the rural-urban migrants in Bihar. In the case of Kerala and urban-urban migrants in Bihar, the proportion of remitters is considerably larger among the bottom 30 per cent of the household income category.

The multiple regression results given in table 10.2 confirm the hypothesis that the smaller the size of household, the greater the capacity to remit only in the case of Uttar Pradesh. They also indicate that the proportion of remitters is, by and large, higher in the case of in-migrants living alone, particularly married ones. Another interesting fact which emerges from the regression results is that the proportion of remitters is smaller among those who have migrated from outside the state in Bihar and higher for the same set in Kerala. There is rather weak evidence (except in the case of Bihar) that the proportion of remitters is higher among those migrating from rural areas than among those from urban areas.

In Bihar, the proportion of remitters is low both among the edu-cated and among the Scheduled Castes/Tribes groups. There is no such evidence in the case of Kerala and Uttar Pradesh. The results also bring out sharply the fact that in Bihar and Uttar Pradesh, not only does the proportion of remitters increase as a function of income but the rate of increase also increases with household income.

Table 10.3 gives us an idea about the magnitude of remittances. It is evident from the table that those who remit money to their places of origin send on average more than one-quarter of their earnings, the proportion of income remitted being about 29 per cent in both Bihar and Uttar Pradesh and about 22 per cent in Kerala. Though

Table 10.1: Percentage of employed in-migrants who had remitted part of their income during the year preceding the survey by demographic and socio-economic characteristics

Characteristics	Bihar		Kerala		Uttar Pradesh	
	Previous place of residence		Previous place of residence		Previous place of residence	
	Rural	Urban	Rural	Urban	Rural	Urban
(N)	(525)	(193)	(283)	(168)	(477)	(156)
All employed in-migrants	25.7	15.0	37.1	32.1	37.1	28.8
Family status						
Married head living alone	73.8	87.5	83.3	100.0	80.0	78.6
Married head living with spouse/children	20.9	8.4	20.4	18.0	26.6	20.0
Unmarried head living alone	41.7	—	73.5	81.8	40.9	—
Others	21.6	10.8	29.4	20.6	37.9	36.4
Years since migration						
0–4 years	26.6	14.3	46.0	40.3	29.9	28.6
5–9 years	28.1	16.2	35.2	33.3	39.5	32.9
10 + years	24.0	14.4	27.5	18.2	38.9	22.7
Education						
No formal education	20.8	—	33.3	—	35.0	34.1
Less than secondary	38.0	21.0	35.9	37.5	41.0	37.4
Secondary	17.7	12.3	45.4	30.9	38.2	36.4
Graduate and above	15.0	13.4	25.8	31.0	28.6	30.1

Religion and caste						
Hindus (excluding Scheduled Castes)	27.5	15.4	33.8	34.9	36.7	27.8
Scheduled Castes/Tribes	15.9	13.6	28.6	80.0*	35.7	44.4
Muslims	26.8	11.1	42.1	30.0	42.9	30.0
Christians	—	—	46.2	20.4	—	—
Employment status						
Self-employed	36.2	10.4	21.4	23.8	15.4	10.7
Wage/salary earner	22.3	16.2	39.0	34.3	40.8	32.8
Land status in previous place of residence						
Landless	25.9	11.9	38.1	31.0	37.4	28.2
Owned land	25.6	21.1	35.3	34.6	36.7	33.3
Household income decile						
Bottom 30 per cent	20.4	27.8	51.9	58.1	31.5	10.2
Middle 40 per cent	28.0	14.1	36.5	31.9	41.7	30.6
Top 30 per cent	27.6	9.9	27.2	16.9	39.3	37.4

* Based on less than 10 observations.

Table 10.2: Estimated regression equations for the determinants of the decision to send remittances by employed in-migrants
(t-values are given in brackets)

Variables		Bihar	Kerala	Uttar Pradesh
HHSZ	Household size	−0.010	0.020+	−0.041**
		(1.43)	(1.76)	(4.48)
MHLD	1 if a married head living with dependants, 0 otherwise	—	—	—
MHLA	1 if a married head living alone, 0 otherwise	0.556**	0.778**	0.442**
		(9.39)	(9.09)	(7.38)
UHIA	1 if an unmarried head living alone, 0 otherwise	0.220*	0.693**	0.044
		(2.01)	(9.81)	(0.45)
SDOH	1 if son/daughter/other relation of head, 0 otherwise	0.073	0.194**	0.271**
		(1.59)	(3.00)	(5.44)
LPRS	1 if an in-migrant from outside the state, 0 otherwise	−0.107**	0.150**	−0.009
		(2.45)	(2.68)	(0.15)
LPRU	1 if an in-migrant from urban areas, O otherwise	−0.061+	−0.025	−0.073
		(1.67)	(0.60)	(1.61)
YRSM	Years since migration	0.004	−0.006	0.009+
		(0.90)	(1.10)	(1.83)
LAND	1 if owned land in previous place of residence, 0 otherwise	0.001	0.075+	0.033
		(0.02)	(1.81)	(0.09)
EDN1	1 if has no formal education, 0 otherwise	—	—	—
EDN2	1 if has less than secondary education, 0 otherwise	0.033	—	0.026
		(0.67)		(0.54)
EDN3	1 if has secondary education, 0 otherwise	−0.138	0.010	0.090+
		(2.56)**	(0.19)	(1.75)
EDN4	1 if a graduate or above, 0 otherwise	−0.165**	−0.085	0.027
		(2.70)	(1.37)	(0.44)
RAC1	1 if a Hindu, 0 otherwise	—	—	—
RAC2	1 if a Scheduled Caste/Tribe 0 otherwise	−0.097**	0.031	0.049
		(2.36)	(0.25)	(0.91)
RAC3	1 if a Muslim, 0 otherwise	−0.027	0.070	0.060
		(0.52)	(0.88)	(1.04)
RAC4	1 if a Christian, 0 otherwise	—	0.053	—
			(1.16)	

Table 10.2 (*Contd.*)

Variables		Bihar	Kerala	Uttar Pradesh
INCM	Income (in 000 Rs)	0.016**	0.015	0.010*
		(3.39)	(1.39)	(2.26)
INCS	Square of income	22.948*@	29.898@	10.120*@
		(2.25)	(0.94)	(1.97)
	Constant	0.170	− 0.037	0.249
	R²	0.228	0.303	0.196
	F	13.690	13.122	10.749
	(N)	(710)	(469)	(677)

@ Figures in 10^{-5}.
** Significant at 1 per cent level.
* Significant at 5 per cent level.
+ Significant at 10 per cent level.

there is no perceptible difference in the proportion of income remitted between different socio-economic groups, the average amount of remittances does provide some interesting results.

It is obvious from the table that on average remittances are significantly higher in Bihar than in the other two states. The mean remittances by urban in-migrants are Rs 3,279, Rs 2,355 and Rs 2,282 for Bihar, Kerala and Uttar Pradesh respectively. In all three states, by and large, mean remittances increase with length of stay in the city. In all three states, mean remittances were also found to increase with educational level. It may be noted here that though the proportion of remitters is low among graduates in Bihar (as seen earlier), the average amount remitted by them is the highest. Remitters among the Scheduled Castes/Tribes in both Bihar and Uttar Pradesh remit on average less than the other caste and religious groups, obviously because of their lower levels of income. In Kerala, however, the highest mean remittances come from the Scheduled Caste/Tribe group.

With regard to employment status, the self-employed on average remit more than wage earners in both Bihar and Uttar Pradesh. In Kerala, on the other hand, wage earners remit more than the self-employed, possibly because wages are fairly high in Kerala. Those who own land at their place of origin remit more than landless remitters in Bihar, whereas exactly the opposite is the case in Uttar Pradesh and there is almost no difference between these two categories in Kerala. In Bihar and Uttar Pradesh, the remitters among the top 30 per cent of the household income group send more than those

Table 10.3: Mean remittances (in rupees) and percentage of income remitted by employed and remitting in-migrants by demographic and socio-economic characteristics

Characteristics	Bihar		Kerala		Uttar Pradesh	
	Mean remittances	Remittances as % of income	Mean remittances	Remittances as % of income	Mean remittances	Remittances as % of income
All	3 279	29.4	2 355	21.8	2 282	29.1
Family status						
Married head living alone	3 826	36.3	3 356	33.2	2 296	31.0
Married head living with spouse/ children	3 370	25.6	1 759	11.6	2 640	27.9
Unmarried head living alone	3 960	56.1	2 824	28.4	2 211	42.1
Others						
Years since migration						
0–4	2 553	32.9	2 093	22.3	1 873	26.3
5–9	3 314	30.4	2 848	22.9	2 288	30.8
10+	3 529	28.4	2 217	18.8	2 511	29.2
Education						
No formal education	3 259	32.3	—	17.8	1 677	24.0
Less than secondary	3 118	33.0	1 350	20.0	2 205	37.6
Secondary	3 208	27.6	2 697	23.4	2 257	27.6
Graduate and above	4 043	22.7	3 441	23.5	3 320	27.7
Religion and caste						
Hindus (excluding Scheduled Castes)	3 474	29.3	2 230	21.5	2 364	29.5
Scheduled Castes/ Tribes	1 833	24.9	2 867	30.0	1 917	30.4
Muslims	3 536	37.4	2 665	18.2	2 026	22.7
Christians	—	—	2 529	22.2	—	—
Employment status						
Self-employed	4 680	36.9	2 073	12.8	2 823	30.8
Wage/salary earner	4 642	25.3	2 496	23.8	2 226	28.7
Land status in previous place of residence						
Landless	2 240	25.1	2 357	23.3	2 406	28.3
Owned land	3 845	30.9	2 352	19.2	2 090	30.3
Household income decile group						
Bottom 30 per cent	2 329	36.6	1 812	23.7	1 947	36.3
Middle 40 per cent	3 408	33.3	3 259	27.7	2 515	32.2
Top 30 per cent	3 986	22.5	1 733	14.6	2 562	29.8

Table 10.3 (*Contd.*)

Characteristics	Bihar		Kerala		Uttar Pradesh	
	Mean remittances	Remittances as % of income	Mean remittances	Remittances as % of income	Mean remittances	Remittances as % of income
Previous place of residence						
Rural	3 219	28.9	2 276	23.2	2 012	32.1
Urban	3 559	33.1	2 511	21.4	3 338	31.9

Table 10.4: Effect of remittances on the level and distribution of household income of in-migrants

	No. of households	Household income	Household income excluding remittances	Percentage change
Mean household income				
Bihar	848	15 776	15 024	− 4.8
Kerala	662	18 951	18 053	− 4.7
Uttar Pradesh	827	11 200	10 253	− 8.5
Distribution of income (Gini coefficient)				
Bihar	848	0.289	0.303	+ 4.8
Kerala	662	0.200	0.228	+ 14.0·
Uttar Pradesh	827	0.425	0.491	+ 15.5

among the bottom 30 per cent. In Kerala, it is the remitters among the bottom 30 per cent who remit more. In Bihar and Uttar Pradesh, remitters from the urban-urban migrant set remit more than rural-urban migrants. The reverse is the case in Kerala.

Table 10.4 shows the effect of remittances on the distribution of income among in-migrant households. Even though both the proportion of remitters and the mean remittances have been noted to be higher among the richer in-migrants, the proportion of income remitted by those remitting from the bottom 30 per cent of the household income category is higher in all three states than that from the top 30 per cent (table 10.3). It may therefore be expected that income distribution among in-migrant households will worsen. There is some evidence of this in the change in the Gini coefficients given in table 10.4. Of course, the worsening in income distribution has not been uniform. Kerala and Uttar Pradesh show a greater degree of inequality on account of remittances than Bihar.

CHAPTER 11

MIGRATION AND THE LEVEL AND DISTRIBUTION OF URBAN HOUSEHOLD INCOME

Table 11.1 provides data on household income and its distribution by migration and income status groups. It is evident from the table that on average annual household income is highest in Kerala and lowest in Uttar Pradesh. The average income for in-migrant households is Rs 15,777, Rs 18,951 and Rs 11,200 for Bihar, Kerala and Uttar Pradesh respectively. The corresponding average household income for non-migrants is Rs 13,741, Rs 16,936 and Rs 13,138. It will be seen that in Bihar and Kerala in-migrants are doing better than non-migrants, whereas in Uttar Pradesh the natives are doing better. With regard to years since migration, there is some evidence of improvement in average household income in Kerala but there seems to be no perceptible change in the other two states.

The measuring of income inequalities in terms of the Gini coefficient brings out some interesting results. Both in Bihar and Kerala, non-migrant households show a more unequal distribution of income than in-migrant households. It is also evident that this difference is much more pronounced in Kerala than in Bihar. In Uttar Pradesh however, it is the in-migrant households which show a more unequal distribution of income.

The distribution of household income by source of income is presented in table 11.2. Taking both in-migrant and non-migrant households, it will be seen that in Bihar and Uttar Pradesh, wage income accounts for around three-quarters of total household income, whereas in Kerala it accounts for only a two-thirds share. In all three states the proportionate share of wage income is higher for in-migrant households than for non-migrant households. It will also be evident from the table that the share of wage income declines with duration of stay in the city in the case of Uttar Pradesh and Kerala, but there seems to be hardly any perceptible change in Bihar. The other important

Table 11.1: Percentage distribution of household income by income groups

State/income decile groups	In-migrant households				Non-migrants
	Years since migration				
	0–4	*5–9*	*10+*	*All*	
Bihar					
Bottom 30 per cent	9.9	10.1	10.2	10.1	10.7
Middle 40 per cent	32.9	30.8	34.6	31.2	33.0
Top 30 per cent	57.2	59.1	55.2	58.7	56.3
Mean household income	13 459	17 326	13 953	15 777	13 741
Gini coefficient	0.321	0.326	0.327	0.332	0.428
Kerala					
Bottom 30 per cent	9.7	10.2	9.5	9.8	9.6
Middle 40 per cent	34.2	33.9	33.8	33.9	32.6
Top 30 per cent	56.1	55.9	56.7	56.3	57.6
Mean household income	18 447	18 838	20 181	18 951	16 936
Gini coefficient	0.283	0.293	0.261	0.282	0.448
Uttar Pradesh					
Bottom 30 per cent	11.6	12.7	12.3	12.0	11.8
Middle 40 per cent	29.8	32.6	30.7	30.6	30.6
Top 30 per cent	58.6	54.7	57.0	57.4	57.6
Mean household income	12 855	9 874	10 482	11 200	13 138
Gini coefficient	0.426	0.396	0.463	0.433	0.336

source of income, i.e. non-farm enterprise, accounts for a 16 per cent share of household income in Bihar and Uttar Pradesh while in Kerala it accounts for only 11 per cent. In all three states, however, the share of income from non-farm enterprise is lower for in-migrant households than for non-migrant households. The relatively low share of income from wage employment and non-farm enterprise among non-migrant households in Kerala arises from the fact that remittances and gifts account for 19 per cent of their income, which is a very high figure compared to the other two states. This suggests that remittances from migrants, particularly to Gulf countries, have made a large contribution to household income in Kerala. The other interesting point to note is that the share of income from rents is three times higher in Kerala and Uttar Pradesh than in Bihar so far as non-migrant households are concerned. Even in the case of in-migrant households,

**Table 11.2: Percentage distribution of household
income by source of income**

State/income decile groups	In-migrant households				Non-migrants
	Years since migration				
	0–4	*5–9*	*10+*	*All*	
Bihar					
Wage employment	82.0	72.3	92.4	76.9	74.0
Farming	5.1	4.6	3.6	4.7	4.2
Non-farm enterprise	11.9	12.8	1.1*	11.8	18.5
Rents	0.0	0.2	1.0	0.2	1.0
Remittances and gifts	0.3	0.5	1.0	0.5	0.8
Others	0.7	9.6	0.9	5.9	1.5
Kerala					
Wage employment	85.8	80.9	79.8	82.8	57.1
Farming	1.4	2.1	3.4	2.1	2.6
Non-farm enterprise	5.6	11.0	10.6	8.4	12.3
Rents	1.8	1.6	2.8	2.0	3.0
Remittances and gifts	2.8	2.4	1.2	2.3	19.4
Others	2.6	2.0	2.2	2.4	5.6
Uttar Pradesh					
Wage employment	83.2	87.2	78.4	83.3	72.1
Farming	3.6	1.8	1.5	2.5	0.6
Non-farm enterprise	9.6	9.5	17.9	11.6	19.6
Rents	0.8	0.1	1.1	0.6	3.0
Remittances and gifts	1.8	0.8	0.2	1.1	2.3
Others	1.0	0.6	0.9	0.9	2.4

* Based on a relatively small number of observations.

in Kerala, the share of rent is distinctly higher than that ror in-migrant households in the other two states.

Table 11.3 provides multiple regression results for the determinants of household income. As expected, household income in all three states remains an increasing function of the number of workers in the household and their educational level. A higher percentage of household workers in the formal sector also results in higher household income. The results show that the higher the proportion of women workers in the household, the lower is the household income, obviously because women are generally paid less. In all three states, Scheduled Caste/Tribe households were found to have a lower average income than the others. Muslims in Bihar also have a lower average income than Hindus, but this is not the case in Uttar Pradesh.

Table 11.3: Estimated regression equations for the determinants of household income (Dependent variable: log of income) (t-values are given in brackets)

Variables		Bihar	Kerala	Uttar Pradesh
NWHH	Number of workers in household (weighted for age)	0.210** (16.64)	0.207** (20.15)	0.216** (25.72)
EDNH	Proportion of household members having secondary or more education	0.163** (6.61)	0.264** (11.52)	0.227** (14.09)
PWGE	Percentage of wage earners	0.001* (2.21)	46.645@ (0.40)	− 0.001** (3.69)
PEFS	Percentage of workers in formal sector	0.002** (11.76)	0.002** (10.75)	0.001* (9.68)
PFMW	Percentage of females among workers	− 0.002** (4.00)	− 0.001** (4.00)	− 0.002** (8.94)
PWAT	Percentage of workers in administrative/ technical job	0.001** (5.06)	0.001** (5.21)	0.002** (8.80)
RCH1	1 if a Hindu household, 0 otherwise	—	—	—
RCH2	1 if a Scheduled Caste/ Tribe household, 0 otherwise	− 0.103** (5.11)	− 0.100** (2.64)	− 0.040** (2.48)
RCH3	1 if a Muslim household, 0 otherwise	− 0.089** (4.02)	0.056** (2.72)	− 0.014 (0.80)
RCH4	1 if a Christian household, 0 otherwise	—	0.044** (3.06)	—
NNMG	1 if a non-migrant household, 0 otherwise	—		
YMH1	1 if head in-migrated in last 0–4 years, 0 otherwise	− 0.056 (0.56)	− 0.371** (4.09)	− 0.086 (1.35)
YMH2	1 if head in-migrated in last 5–9 years, 0 otherwise	0.179* (2.32)	− 0.038 (0.39)	− 0.083 (1.54)
YMH3	1 if head in-migrated 10 + years ago, 0 otherwise	− 0.063 (1.23)	0.012 (0.12)	− 0.049 (1.03)
EDM1	Interaction of EDNH and YMH1	0.044 (1.47)	0.056** (2.42)	0.001 (0.06)
EDM2	Interaction of EDNH and YMH2	− 0.003 (0.13)	0.020 (0.68)	− 0.006 (0.41)
EDM3	Interaction of EDNH and YMH3	0.073** (4.09)	0.046 (1.39)	− 0.049 (0.03)
WGM1	Interaction of PWGE and YMH1	− 0.001 (1.28)	0.002** (2.54)	0.001 (1.20)

Table 11.3 (*Contd.*)

Variables		Bihar	Kerala	Uttar Pradesh
WGM2	Interaction of PWGE and YMH2	− 0.001** (2.78)	13.376@ (1.03)	0.001 (1.10)
WGM3	Interaction of PWGE and YMH3	0.001* (2.02)	− 0.001 (1.68) +	12.513 (0.25)
ATM1	Interaction of PWAT and YMH1	0.001 (0.13)	26.602@ (0.43)	0.001 (0.98)
ATM2	Interaction of PWAT and YMH2	31.674@ (0.55)	34.199@ (0.76)	0.001 (0.81)
ATM3	Interaction of PWAT and YMH3	20.387@ (1.02)	− 0.001 + (1.84)	0.001 (0.68)
	Constant	3.531	3.602	3.627
	R^2	0.334	0.465	0.501
	F	49.213	60.418	94.612
	(N)	(1,981)	(1,480)	(1,903)

@ Coefficients are in 10^{-5}.
** Significant at 1 per cent level.
* Significant at 5 per cent level.
+ Significant at 10 per cent level.

Christians and Muslims in Kerala have a significantly higher average household income than Hindus.

With respect to migrant status, the results show that recent in-migrant households in Bihar have the same level of household income as non-migrant households. However, in-migrant households of 5–10 years' standing have a relatively higher average household income than the natives. This difference disappears in the case of those who migrated more than 10 years ago. In Kerala, recent in-migrant households appear to be at some disadvantage in terms of income, which is not perceptible among in-migrant households of more than 5 years' standing. In Uttar Pradesh, there does not appear to be any statistically significant difference between the average household income of in-migrant and non-migrant households in the multiple regression model.

CHAPTER 12

MIGRATION AND THE AVAILABILITY OF HOUSING AND OTHER AMENITIES

This section is basically about the living conditions in urban areas in general and also of in-migrants compared to non-migrants. Taking both in-migrants and non-migrants, 62 per cent of households in Kerala live in owned dwellings, whereas in Bihar and Uttar Pradesh the percentages are 29 and 22 respectively (see table 12.1). There are, however, perceptible differences between in-migrant and non-migrant households. Whereas the percentages of households owning dwelling are 13, 34 and 10 respectively for in-migrants in Bihar, Kerala and Uttar Pradesh, the corresponding percentages for non-migrants are 40, 80 and 31. Though there is not much evidence of improvement in the situation with respect to years since migration in Bihar or Uttar Pradesh, in Kerala the proportion of households owning dwellings does increase significantly with duration of stay in the city.

Among those owning houses, about half own houses valued at Rs 50,000 and above in all three states. This proportion is, however, higher in the case of in-migrants than non-migrants in Bihar and Kerala, but not in Uttar Pradesh.

With regard to the average land area of dwellings (whether owned or rented), it is highest in Uttar Pradesh and lowest in Kerala. In all three states, the average area of dwellings is lower for in-migrants than for non-migrants. Though there seems to be some improvement among in-migrants with increasing duration of stay in Bihar and Kerala, they still do not appear to catch up with non-migrants in this respect.

The average number of rooms in dwellings is about three in Kerala, two in Bihar and a little less than two in Uttar Pradesh. In all three states, this average is lower for in-migrants than for non-migrants. There is thus some congestion in dwellings, particularly in Uttar Pradesh and Bihar. In Bihar the extent of overcrowding is even greater

Table 12.1: Dwelling particulars of households by migration status

| State/dwelling | In-migrant households | | | | Non-migrant households |
| | Years since migration | | | | |
	0–4	5–9	10+	All	
Bihar					
Proportion of households owning their dwellings	12.4	13.6	7.0	12.7	40.1
Proportion of households owning dwellings valued at Rs 50,000 and above	53.6	54.2	66.7	54.4	33.7
Average land area of dwellings (sq. m.)	105	135	125	123	146
Average number of rooms in dwellings	2.07	2.12	2.13	2.10	2.34
Kerala					
Proportion of households owning their dwellings	19.3	43.4	53.4	34.3	79.6
Proportion of households owning dwellings valued at Rs 50,000 and above	55.0	59.6	59.0	58.1	41.8
Average land area of dwellings (sq. m.)	59	66	68	63	71
Average number of rooms in dwellings	2.56	2.94	3.15	2.81	3.49
Uttar Pradesh					
Proportion of household owning their dwellings	9.0	9.7	12.1	10.0	30.9
Proportion of households owning dwellings valued at Rs 50,000 and above	46.4	39.3	65.4	50.0	62.3
Average land area of dwellings (sq. m.)	232	175	204	205	287
Average number of rooms in dwellings	1.59	1.37	1.45	1.48	2.00

when we consider the average household size—5.4, 4.9 and 4.8 household members in Bihar, Kerala and Uttar Pradesh respectively.

It will be seen from table 12.2 that there is a considerable dearth of basic civic amenities in the urban centres. In Bihar, among in-migrant households, 23 per cent do not have electricity and 12 per cent use non-piped water for drinking. The respective percentages for non-

Table 12.2: Particulars about facilities available in the dwelling by migration status

State/facilities available in dwelling	In-migrant households				Non-migrant households
	Years since migration				
	0–4	*5–9*	*10+*	*All*	
Bihar					
Proportion of households having					
Electricity	77.4	75.3	85.7	76.7	66.0
Separate kitchen	71.4	72.9	77.2	72.7	60.2
Separate bathroom	55.0	59.7	57.9	58.0	49.5
Proportion of households having drinking water from					
Piped water inside dwelling	61.4	64.5	66.7	63.6	56.8
Piped water outside dwelling	28.3	22.3	28.1	24.7	26.3
Pukka well	0.7	0.0	0.0	0.2	1.3
Other sources	9.6	13.2	5.2	11.5	15.6
Kerala					
Proportion of households having					
Electricity	97.7	96.1	95.8	96.8	85.7
Separate kitchen	82.3	93.2	91.0	87.6	94.8
Separate bathroom	85.9	90.7	87.5	87.7	79.8
Proportion of households having drinking water from					
Piped water inside dwelling	86.1	84.4	84.6	85.3	55.2
Piped water outside dwelling	10.6	13.2	11.5	11.7	38.7
Pukka well	1.9	2.5	2.8	2.3	5.4
Other sources	1.4	0.0	1.1	0.7	0.7
Uttar Pradesh					
Proportion of households having					
Electricity	69.1	58.0	56.3	61.9	73.6
Separate kitchen	37.5	22.2	30.2	30.3	50.7
Separate bathroom	29.3	23.3	38.1	30.6	52.6
Proportion of households having drinking water from					
Piped water inside dwelling	46.0	37.2	39.5	41.2	55.3
Piped water outside dwelling	23.1	21.9	26.0	23.5	17.1
Pukka well	4.6	4.5	2.4	4.0	3.6
Other sources	26.3	36.4	32.1	31.3	24.0

migrants are 34 and 17. In Uttar Pradesh, among in-migrants, about 38 per cent do not have electricity and about 35 per cent do not have piped water for drinking. The corresponding percentages for non-migrants are 26 and 28. In Kerala, among in-migrants, 3 per cent do not have electricity and 3 per cent again do not have piped water for drinking; the corresponding percentages for non-migrants are 14 and 6. Thus poor living conditions are to be found in both Bihar and Uttar Pradesh, but more pronounced in Uttar Pradesh. The availability of separate kitchens and bathrooms in dwellings is another indicator of healthy living conditions. In general more than half of all households have both separate kitchen and separate bathroom. In Kerala, however, this percentage is more than 80. In the case of dwellings with a separate kitchen, the figure is around 65, 92 and 42 per cent in Bihar, Kerala and Uttar Pradesh respectively. Except in Bihar, the percentage of dwellings with a separate kitchen is higher among non-migrants than among in-migrants, but the percentage of dwellings with a separate bathroom is higher for in-migrants than in both Bihar and Kerala. It is the other way round in Uttar Pradesh. The relatively better living conditions noticed in Bihar as compared to Uttar Pradesh may be partly attributed to the migration of professionals to work in public sector undertakings in Bokaro Steel City. Though, as noted earlier, there is in general some increase in the proportion of households owning their dwellings with increasing length of stay, there is no perceptible change in other living conditions.

CHAPTER 13

SPECIAL FEATURES OF INTERNATIONAL OUT-MIGRANTS FROM KERALA

The discussion so far has largely concentrated on migration flows within India, except in Sections 3-and 4 where brief references were made to out-migration from the rural areas of Kerala to Gulf countries. The present section gives a brief account of the special features of international migration from both rural and urban areas of Kerala.

Data on the profile of international out-migrants are presented in table 13.1. As regards out-migrants from rural areas, it is clear that they are largely male, semi-skilled workers with less than secondary education in the 20–44 age group. About one-third of these out-migrants were employed before migration, so they at least had some work experience before migration. Those who were students before out-migrating (4 per cent) may be treated as inexperienced workers, but the two-thirds who reported being unemployed before migration were possibly not first time job seekers in view of the fact that most of them belong to the 20–44 age group. The profile of the out-migrants from urban areas indicates that the process of selectivity with respect to sex, age and marital status is similar to that in the rural areas. But there are noticeable differences between the two groups with respect to their religion, caste, education and pre-migration activity status. Muslims and Hindus have a relatively higher propensity to out-migrate from rural areas, whereas Muslims and Christians show a greater proneness to out-migrate from urban areas. The educational level of out-migrants from the urban areas is relatively higher than that of out-migrants from the rural areas. These better educated out-migrants from the urban areas also tend to be more experienced than their rural counterparts, as is indicated by the fact that a larger proportion (nearly two-thirds) of them were employed before migration.

Table 13.1: Percentage distribution of international out-migrants from Kerala by demographic and socio-economic characteristics and previous place of residence

Characteristics	Previous place of residence			
	Rural		Urban	
	International out-migrants	General population	International out-migrants	General population
(N)	(429)	(9 829)	(225)	(6 047)
Relation to head				
Head	16.8	35.1	19.6	27.1
Son/daughter	59.9	47.6	66.2	51.5
Others	23.3	17.3	14.2	21.4
Sex				
Male	92.5	50.6	85.8	49.5
Female	7.5	49.4	14.2	50.5
Age at migration (years)				
10–19	3.3	27.8	0.5	24.0
20–29	64.6	23.9	63.7	18.6
30–44	30.4	20.7	32.3	14.2
45 +	1.5	26.5	3.5	21.6
Marital status				
Married	43.5	54.5	45.5	59.8
Unmarried	56.5	45.5	54.5	40.2
Religion and caste				
Hindus (excluding Schedle Castes)	58.3	49.9	35.1	48.9
Scheduled Castes) Tribes	2.8	8.1	1.8	3.5
Christians	9.1	29.5	23.1	18.8
Muslims	29.8	12.4	40.0	28.7
Education before migration				
No formal education	0.5	17.6	0.5	4.8
Less than secondary	73.7	62.6	40.0	60.3
Secondary	15.4	15.1	33.0	24.1
Graduate and above	10.5	4.7	26.5	10.7
Activity status before migration				
Employed	34.3	27.5	62.0	21.0
Unemployed	60.2	18.2	30.5	7.6
Student	4.1	21.5	5.5	31.6
Others	1.4	32.8	2.0	39.7

**Table 13.2: Percentage of remitters among employed
international out-migrants and mean remittances
(in rupees) per remitter by demographic and socio-economic
characteristics and previous place of residence**

Characteristics	Previous place of residence			
	Rural		Urban	
	Percentage remitters	Mean remittances (Rs)	Percentage remitters	Mean remittances (Rs)
All				
	93.1	8 428	87.4	19 109
Relation to head of household				
Head	100.0	10 766	95.1	22 667
Son/daughter	92.0	8 626	86.5	18 399
Others	90.1	8 376	78.3	13 971
Sex				
Male	94.0	8 965	87.8	19 235
Female	55.6	15 108*	77.8	16 012
Age at migration (years)				
10–19	90.9	9 175	—	—
20–29	94.5	8 503	86.4	19 583
30–44	90.9	8 839	89.1	17 122
45 +	83.3	10 947	85.7	22 365
Marital status				
Married	90.6	8 785	85.6	19 745
Unmarried	95.6	8 273	90.4	18 512
Religion and caste				
Hindus (excluding Scheduled Castes)	92.4	9 827	77.8	22 365
Scheduled Castes/ Tribes	100.0	6 812	—	—
Christians	80.8	12 470	93.8	15 127
Muslims	96.6	10 232	91.0	19 738
Education before migration				
No formal education	—	—	—	—
Less than secondary	94.0	8 653	89.7	12 843
Secondary	91.9	9 955	93.2	16 836
Graduate and above	84.6	14 668	76.5	36 233

* Figures based on less than 10 observations.

The data related to remittance behaviour, as presented in table 13.2, indicate that nearly all employed international out-migrants send remittances home, irrespective of whether they have out-migrated from rural or urban areas. The proportion of remitters is noticeably low only in the case of female out-migrants from the rural areas, possibly because they are accompanied by their husbands and do not remit separately.

Although there is not much difference in the proportion of remitters between out-migrants from rural and urban areas or among different socio-economic groups, there is a significant difference in the size of their remittances. On average, out-migrants from rural areas send Rs 8,428 per year as against Rs 19,109 sent by out-migrants from urban areas. The latter therefore send nearly two and a half times as much as the former. This is perhaps due to the fact that out-migrants from rural areas are mostly semi-skilled workers with relatively low incomes, while those from urban areas with more education are earning more. Among the out-migrants, heads of household, on average, remit more than other household members. The size of remittances is also higher for relatively more educated out-migrants than for the less educated. The data show that graduate out-migrants from urban areas send on average more than Rs 36,000 per year.

CHAPTER 14

SUMMARY OF MAJOR FINDINGS
AND THEIR POLICY IMPLICATIONS

The present study has examined migration flows and their implications in the three selected states of India—Bihar, Kerala and Uttar Pradesh. The socio-economic profile of the three states, based on secondary data and presented in Chapter 2, indicate that Bihar is deep in a quagmire of non-development, whereas signs of economic growth are visible both in Kerala and in Uttar Pradesh, particularly industrial growth in Kerala and agricultural growth in Uttar Pradesh. This is also substantiated by the findings of the surveys, carried out as part of this study.

The analysis of data on the profile of rural out-migrants and return-migrants, presented in Chapter 3, shows that out-migration flows are relatively higher in Bihar and Uttar Pradesh than in Kerala. Although a process of selectivity with respect to education is in evidence in the out-migration flow in all three states, in Bihar and Uttar Pradesh even those with less than secondary education appear to have a relatively high propensity to out-migrate. This, along with the fact that relatively young (and, therefore, less experienced) persons dominate the out-migration stream in Bihar and Uttar Pradesh, may imply more difficult living conditions in the rural areas of these two states. In all three states, the poor (belonging to the bottom two deciles of household income) and unemployed out-migrate in larger proportions, mainly in search of 'work and income opportunities'. In Bihar, it is the landless who are more prone to migration whereas in Kerala and Uttar Pradesh the landed groups dominate the migration flows. While wage earners dominate the migration flows in Bihar and Kerala, the self-employed and unpaid family workers have a relatively higher propensity to out-migrate in Uttar Pradesh. The evidence of sizeable out-migration even among employed persons in each of the three states (more than 20 per cent in Uttar Pradesh, an agriculturally fairly prosperous region with 97 per cent of households using irrigation) suggests the existence of high levels of under-employment and disguised unemployment. Lack of employment and poor earnings were in fact given as important reasons for out-migrating by a large proportion of out-migrants. Rural out-migration thus appears to be largely a survival strategy for quite a large number of out-migrants. The higher propensity to out-migrate observed in Bihar and Uttar Pradesh may be explained partly in terms of the more intolerable living conditions in the rural areas of these two states. Though quite a sizeable proportion (more than 30 per cent) of out-migrants in Bihar and Uttar Pradesh are self-employed, the majority of them end up as wage/salary earners after migration.

The out-migration flow is also associated with a return-migration flow, since out-migrants often return to their places of origin. The evidence suggests that the rate of return-migration is about 1 per cent in Bihar and Uttar Pradesh, and about 2 per cent in Kerala. The relatively high rate of return-migration in Kerala is due to the return of migrants from the Gulf countries. The breakdown of data on reasons for returning show that the majority of migrants return on retirement or completion of contract work (as in the case of Kerala), or because of dissatisfaction with the working and living conditions in their places of destination (as in the case of Bihar). Nevertheless, the evidence suggests that many return-migrants do bring back some skills and resources. Return-migrants in Bihar appear, however, to perform less well in this respect than those in the other two states.

The data on the in-flow of resources to the rural areas through remittances from out-migrants, presented in Chapter 4, show that the proportion of remitters is fairly high—72, 67 and 47 per cent of Bihar, Kerala and Uttar Pradesh respectively. The fact that the proportion of remitters is lowest in Uttar Pradesh and highest in Bihar may suggest that the need of out-migrant households for remittances is much higher in agriculturally poor regions like Bihar and Kerala. There is not much difference in the proportion of remitters between those who go to rural areas and those who go to urban areas. The overall proportion of remitters is large in all three states, partly because a large majority of out-migrants who go in search of 'employment and income' singly, leaving their families behind in poverty, feel compelled to remit something back home. It is important to note in this context that the percentage of households from which only one member has out-migrated is high in all three states—86, 66 and 71 per cent in Bihar, Kerala and Uttar Pradesh respectively.

In all three states, the proportion of remitters is lower among those with no formal education than among those with some formal education. It is also generally lower among the landless than among the landed in Uttar Pradesh, but the trend is reversed in Bihar and Kerala. The proportion of remitters, by and large, increases as a function of years since migration, particularly in Bihar and Uttar Pradesh. This may indicate a rather long period of settling down, which is perhaps a reflection on the difficult living and working conditions facing out-migrants from those two states. This, together with the fact that a fairly high proportion of those who out-migrated more than 10 years ago are still remitting, may suggest both the continuing need of the parent households for remittances and the desire of out-migrants to keep their links intact because of uncertain and difficult conditions at their present place of residence. In all three states, the size of remittances is higher for out-migrants from cultivating as compared with non-cultivating households, for wage/salary earners than for the self-employed, and for out-migrants who go to the urban areas than for those who go to the rural areas. The data show that remittances are received by all income classes among out-migrant households, although the poorer groups receive more, on average, in all three states. The results also show that the size of remittances increases with the level of education of the out-migrants in the case of Bihar. This is understandable because education is a proxy for income, so with increasing levels of education the capacity of out-migrants to remit also increases. But it is interesting to note that there is no such trend in Kerala or Uttar Pradesh. This may be because the less educated from Uttar Pradesh, who come from relatively poor households, feel a greater compulsion to send more, while the out-migrants to Gulf countries from Kerala, though less educated, earn more. As expected, the size of remittances also increases with years since migration in all three states.

The impact of remittances on the incomes of out-migrant households has been far from marginal. The incomes of out-migrant households, on average, increase by 48, 74 and 25 per cent in Bihar, Kerala and Uttar Pradesh respectively. What is important to note in this context is that the poorer out-migrant households benefit relatively more from remittances, which is reflected in the reduction in inequality in household income distribution among out-migrant households in all three states.

More than half of the households receiving remittances spend them on household goods, food and clothing. However, about 9 per cent of cultivating households receiving remittances in Uttar Pradesh also spend them on productive investment. Expenditure on education also has some importance in Bihar and Uttar Pradesh.

In Chapter 5, the analysis of the effects of migration on production and agricultural technology brings out several important points. The rate of adoption of HYV is highest among return-migrant households, followed by out-migrant households. This pattern is fairly consistent across the three states. With respect to the use of costly modern implements (like tractor, thresher and tubewell), the pattern is not uniform in the three states. In Bihar, the use of such implements is highest among out-migrant households who receive remittances. In Kerala and Uttar Pradesh, their use is highest among out-migrant households who do not receive remittances. This is perhaps due to the fact that relatively more out-migrants in these two states come from richer households. The use of modern implements is higher among return-migrant than among out-migrant households. The data on improved agricultural practices show that a relatively large percentage of migrant households, taking out-migrants and return-migrants together, use them as compared with non-migrant households. The differences between the out-migrant and return-migrant households are not, however, uniform: while in some cases the out-migrant households show better performance, in others it is the return-migrants.

The data on irrigation show that the proportion of agricultural households using irrigation from all sources is much higher than that from tubewells alone. This indicates that the level of infrastructural support is fairly weak in all three states. It is also interesting to note that the intensity of cropping is as low as 103 and 120 in Bihar and Uttar Pradesh respectively. Given the fact that the proportion of households using irrigation in these two states is quite high (61 and 97 per cent in Bihar and Uttar Pradesh respectively), one cannot fail to conclude that irrigation in these states is more 'protective' than 'productive'. With regard to migrant status, a relatively large percentage of return-migrant and out-migrant households use irrigation as compared with non-migrant households.

A comparison between migrant and non-migrant households with respect to land productivity indicates that it is highest among return-migrant households, followed by out-migrant households, and lowest among non-migrant households, in all three states. Land productivity is lowest (almost pathetic) in Bihar and highest in Kerala (even with the lowest level of irrigation of the three states), for all households taken together. This perhaps suggests that the infrastructural support (particularly power, credit and extension services) is weaker in Bihar and Uttar Pradesh than in Kerala. As regards labour productivity, the data show that it is higher among out-migrant and return-migrant households. Here again labour productivity in general is lowest in Bihar and highest in Kerala.

The analysis of the effects of migration on the employment situation in rural areas shows that migration has led to some improvement only in Kerala. The analysis also shows that, in all three states, the loss of labour due to the out-migration of household member(s) is partly compensated for by increased use of hired labour and partly by increased participation of women in work. The loss of out-migrants' labour, therefore, does not appear to cause a decrease either in labour or land productivity; these have rather increased, giving support to Lewis's thesis of disguised unemployment.

The conclusion that the migration flow contributes to land productivity, particularly in the case of return-migrants, is also borne out by the results of multiple regression analysis. The results also indicate the positive role of the resource and information inflow in enhancing land productivity, in the case of both return-migrant and out-migrant households. One can unhesitatingly conclude, therefore, that the migration process does make some contribution towards increasing land and labour productivity. However, the positive impact of out-migration and return-migration does not appear to have been fully realized because of weak infrastructural development in the rural areas.

The analysis of urban survey data is presented in Chapters 6–12. The characteristics of urban in-migrants, as discussed in Chapter 6, show that in all three states, in-migrants are relatively younger than the natives. In Bihar and Kerala, on the whole, in-migrants also tend to be more educated than the natives. In Uttar Pradesh, the proportion of in-migrants with 'no formal education' is much higher among those who come from rural areas than among those from the urban areas or natives. This may be because the expansion taking place in the old industrial city of Kanpur requires unskilled labourers like loaders, head-load carriers and semi-skilled workers from village groups (leather tanning workers, cobblers, blacksmiths, carpenters, etc.).

The examination of data on the socio-economic characteristics of urban in-migrants at the time of migration reveals certain important facts. Besides students, those who were unemployed before migration constitute a sizeable proportion of in-migrants from both rural and urban areas. This is sharply reflected in the reasons for migration given at the time of interview. Excluding in-migrants who either follow or accompany the family (which is quite sizeable, about 40 per cent, and fairly evenly distributed among states), the large bulk of in-migrants in all three states come for employment or better employment, either in terms of more working days or more remuneration. This finding is consistent with those of the rural survey, where a large majority of rural out-migrants indicated that the search for employment or better employment was the reason for out-migration. When asked about reasons for moving to the city, most in-migrants answered that 'rozi roti ke liye aye hain', which means 'we have come to earn our bread'.

Among in-migrants who looked for work after migration, 71, 96 and 64 per cent found employment within three months of their arrival in Bihar, Kerala and Uttar Pradesh respectively. In Kerala, nearly all those with no formal education got absorbed within three months of in-migration. Those with some education had to wait a little longer, but nearly all got their first job within a year. There was, however, not much difference in the waiting period between migrants from rural and urban areas. On the other hand, the process of absorption in the urban labour market is slower in both Bihar and Uttar Pradesh. Almost 5 per cent of in-migrants in Bihar and about 15 per cent in Uttar Pradesh had to wait more than a year for their first job. Further, in-migrants from urban areas had to wait a little longer than those from rural areas. Again, in Bihar and Uttar Pradesh as in Kerala, in-migrants with some education had to wait slightly longer than those with no formal education. These results, in general, suggest that the urban labour markets in Bihar and Uttar Pradesh have a lower absorptive capacity and are perhaps poorly organized compared with those in Kerala.

The comparison of employment status before and after migration shows that, on the whole, there is a notable shift from self-employment to wage employment. The shift is more pronounced in Bihar and Uttar Pradesh, for in-migrants from both rural and urban areas. In Kerala, where relatively more workers are in wage employment even before migration, the shift is relatively smaller. With respect to improvements in income, the analysis shows that almost three-quarters of in-migrants in Bihar and Kerala and about half in Uttar Pradesh are able to improve their income soon after migration. In Bihar, almost 50 per cent of in-migrants from rural areas and 30 per cent of those from urban areas are able to more than double their income. The corresponding percentages for Kerala and Uttar Pradesh are significantly lower. This indicates that rural-urban income differentials are relatively larger in Bihar than in Kerala or Uttar Pradesh.

Labour force participation rates among in-migrants and non-migrants, presented in Chapter 7, show that in-migrants have a relatively higher labour force participation rate than non-migrants, particularly in the case of the younger age groups (10–24 years), in all three states. This may suggest that many of the relatively young in-migrants, who should be going to school, have no option but to work to supplement their family income, because of poverty. Further, the participation rate is generally higher among in-migrants from rural areas compared with those from urban areas. This difference is partly explained by the fact that women in-migrants from rural areas have a relatively higher participation rate than those from urban areas; secondly, the Scheduled Castes/Tribes, who generally have a higher participation rate, constitute a larger proportion among in-migrants from rural areas than among those from urban areas. In Bihar, which suffers from acute poverty, it was found that the labour force participation rate is higher if the household owns an enterprise, probably because it can make use of women and young family members as workers. The negative association of participation rate with per capita income for the 10–24 age group in all three states suggests that those in the higher income brackets prefer to have their children educated rather than sending them to work.

Chapter 8 is concerned with the analysis of the structure of employment and unemployment, and with the assimilation of migrants into the urban labour market. The results show that the public sector is responsible for two-thirds of total wage employment in Bihar (because of the public sector steel plant in Bokaro), and a little less than half in Kerala and Uttar Pradesh. Though there is not much difference in the share of public sector employment between in-migrants and non-migrants, the share is lower among recent in-migrants (0–4 years' standing) as compared with those of longer standing. It is also evident that a sizeable proportion of in-migrants initially get absorbed in the informal sector; while many of them improve their position and eventually get absorbed in the formal sector, a large proportion remain in the informal sector for years to come. Thus about one-third of wage-earning in-migrants in Bihar and Kerala, and more than half in Uttar Pradesh, remain part of the informal sector, where factory acts and labour laws related to even such crucial matters as hours of work or minimum wages are not operative. The share in formal sector employment of in-migrants compared with non-migrants is almost the same in Bihar, slightly larger in Kerala, and much smaller in Uttar Pradesh.

It is also evident that unemployment is more acute among non-migrants than among in-migrants; and among the educated than among those with no formal education, although a sizeable proportion of unemployed graduates, both in-migrants and non-migrants, are prepared to work for less than Rs 500 a month. The percentages of the unemployed who had been looking for a job for more than a year were 78, 56 and 34 per cent in Bihar, Uttar Pradesh and Kerala respectively. This may have contributed to increasing criminalization in urban centres.

The analysis of data on urban earnings in Chapter 9 provides some important conclusions. The mean income per employed person is lower for in-migrants than for non-migrants in Bihar and Uttar Pradesh, but it is the other way round in Kerala. Among both in-migrants and non-migrants, wage/salary earners have a higher income than the self-employed in Bihar, whereas self-employed people earn more, on average, than wage/salary earners in both Kerala and Uttar Pradesh. With regard to previous place of residence, those coming from urban areas do not have significantly different incomes from non-migrants. But in-migrants from the rural areas are at a disadvantage vis-à-vis non-migrants. In Bihar, this disadvantage is noticed in the case of wage earners only, but in the other two states, among both wage earners and the self-employed, in-migrants from rural areas earn less than non-migrants. With increasing duration of stay, in-migrants generally are able to improve their earnings.

Chapter 10 is designed to complement Chapter 4, looking at the scale and determinants of remittances sent by urban in-migrants and the effects of remittances on urban household income distribution. The data show that the percentage of remitters among employed in-migrants is about 23 per cent in Bihar and 35 per cent in both Kerala and Uttar Pradesh. In all three states, the percentage of remitters is higher among migrants from rural areas than among those from urban areas. This suggests that migrants from rural areas are under a greater compulsion to remit, partly because of abject poverty in the rural areas and partly because of their desire to maintain ties with their families. The percentage of remitters among Scheduled Castes/Tribes is relatively high both in Kerala and Uttar Pradesh but not in Bihar. The relatively low proportion of remitters among Scheduled Castes/Tribes in Bihar is due to their generally lower levels of income. In both Bihar and Uttar Pradesh, the proportion of remitters is found to increase as a function of income, which is indicative of the poor remitting capacity of in-migrants in the lower income brackets. In spite of the generally low average incomes of the remitters, as discussed in Chapter 9, the need for remittances among the parent households is perhaps so great that the remitters, by and large, send home almost one-quarter of their income. Not only is the proportion of income remitted relatively higher in Bihar and Uttar Pradesh than in Kerala, but the mean remittances are also higher in these two states. The data also show that among in-migrants the proportion of income remitted by those from poorer households is greater than that remitted by those from richer households. Income distribution among in-migrant households thus worsens as a consequence of remittances.

Chapter 11 is an attempt to examine the effects of migration on the level and distribution of household income in the urban areas. A comparison between the three states shows that the average household income is highest in Kerala and lowest in Uttar Pradesh. The mean household income for in-migrants is Rs 15,777, Rs 18,951 and Rs 11,200 in Bihar, Kerala and Uttar Pradesh respectively. The corresponding figures for non-migrants are Rs 13,741, Rs 16,936 and Rs 13,138. In the case of rural household income (discussed in Chapter 4), the highest mean household income is also registered by Kerala but the lowest by Bihar. Of course, rural-urban differentials are very large in all three states. It is also worth noting that the differences in the level of household income between states are more pronounced as regards rural income than urban income, which suggests that regional unevenness in development is perhaps more pronounced in rural than in urban India.[1]

[1] Such a conclusion is likely to hold even if regional price differentials are taken into account.

In Bihar and Kerala, as noted above, the average income of urban in-migrant households is higher than that of native households, while it is the other way round in Uttar Pradesh. Both in Bihar and Kerala, income distribution among non-migrant households is more unequal than among in-migrant households. In Uttar Pradesh, however, income inequality is greater among in-migrant households.

The results of the regression analysis show that urban household income, in all three states, increases as a function of the number of workers in the household, the proportion of wage/salary earners to total workers in the household, the average level of education of the household workers, and the percentage of household workers in the formal sector. On the other hand, average household income decreases as a function of the proportion of women workers in the household. The results also indicate that Scheduled Caste/Tribe households have a lower mean income than households belonging to other religious/caste groups.

The availability of housing and other amenities in urban centres, as discussed in Chapter 12, shows that not many households own their dwellings in Bihar and Uttar Pradesh, and that the percentage of households owning their dwellings is still lower among in-migrant households than among natives in all three States. The average numbers of rooms in dwellings (owned or rented) is three in Kerala, two in Bihar and a little less than two in Uttar Pradesh. Since the average household size in Bihar is higher (5.4) than in Kerala and Uttar Pradesh (4.9 and 4.8 respectively), the extent of overcrowding appears to be relatively greater in Bihar than in the other two states. In general, more than half of all households have separate kitchens and bathrooms.

The urban survey data also show that there is a considerable lack of basic civic amenities in the urban centres. In Bihar, among in-migrant households, 23 per cent do not have electricity and 12 per cent use non-piped water for drinking. The respective percentages for non-migrant households are 34 and 17. In Uttar Pradesh, among in-migrant households, about 38 per cent do not have electricity and about 35 per cent do not get piped water for drinking. The corresponding percentages for non-migrants are 26 and 28. In Kerala, among in-migrant households, 3 per cent do not have electricity and 3 per cent again do not have piped water; the respective percentages for non-migrant households are 14 and 6. There is thus some evidence of poor living conditions in both Bihar and Uttar Pradesh, but more pronounced in Uttar Pradesh than in Bihar.

The examination of the characteristics of international out-migrants from Kerala in Chapter 13 reveals that international migration flows are dominated more by relatively older and more experienced people. However, there is no evidence of brain drain associated with international migration, particularly to the Gulf countries. The data show that the return-migration flow is higher in the case of international migration as compared with internal migration because most international out-migrants go for a fixed period of employment. The data also show that international migrants send more remittances than internal migrants because of their relatively higher incomes.

The findings of this study, in general, suggest that out-migration from the rural areas is largely a survival strategy. Estimates show that open unemployment among urban in-migrants is 6.3, 23.8 and 9.4 per cent in Bihar, Kerala and Uttar Pradesh respectively. The corresponding figures for non-migrants are 9.7, 39.8 and 14.8 per cent. With such a high rate of urban unemployment, the chances for rural out-migrants to have even minimum standards of living and working conditions in urban areas are indeed low. In fact, the analysis shows that many rural out-migrants face severe unemployment, low wages, and hazardous and poor working conditions in the overcrowded urban informal sector. A fairly long period of waiting for jobs and poor living conditions add to criminalization in the urban centres. But if such people do not out-migrate from the rural areas, their struggle for survival there is likely to result in even more organized violence in the rural areas, possibly throwing the rural areas into utter chaos. Thus, the rural out-migration flow cannot, and indeed, should not, be stopped through direct government intervention. Controlling or reducing the flow of migration will only add to misery and poverty in the rural areas.

However, the finding that a very large proportion of the unemployed are looking for clerical jobs indicates that the structure of the labour supply is not in harmony with the occupational demand for labour. This may therefore suggest that changes in educational and training programmes, changes in attitudes to different kinds of work and more flexible wage structures are needed in India.

The analysis also shows that migration provides some benefits to the rural areas, particularly through the process of remittances. It leads to improvements in land and labour productivity, the adoption of modern agricultural technology, and a reduction in rural income inequalities. These improvements are more pronounced where the flows of remittances and return-migration are greater. The gains to the rural areas would be even more impressive if the rural areas were not starved of infrastructural development, particularly with respect to water management (with emphasis on productive irrigation) and power.

The evidence suggests that in-migrants from rural areas have a greater propensity to remit than those from urban areas, largely because rural-urban migration is more individual than family, as compared with urban-urban migration. In terms of the positive effects of migration on the development of the origin areas, rural-urban migration is thus more beneficial for rural areas than urban-urban migration for urban areas.

The overall use of remittances is, however, heavily consumption-oriented. Whatever is left after consumption is mostly being spent on the purchase of stocks, land and residential buildings. A very small proportion of remittances is being used for productive investment, even in Kerala where the flow of remittances is large and there is no extreme rural poverty. This may be partly because of the generally gloomy prospects for agricultural and industrial development.

The higher participation of women in work activities noticed as a consequence of the out-migration of one or more family members is a positive aspect both from the point of view of enhancing the status of women and in terms of reducing demographic pressures in poor rural areas.

The available evidence suggests that return-migration is higher in Kerala than in Bihar and Uttar Pradesh because of the greater economic diversification in rural Kerala. There is therefore a clear policy option for more regionally balanced public investment in rural areas with a view to building up infrastructural support for agriculture and allied activities, like food processing and preservation and other agro-based rural industries. To begin with, this will require substantial public investment in water management, for efficient use and development of productive irrigation potential, land reclamation and power. Tenancy reforms are also needed to weaken the semi-feudal structure which is another big obstacle to rural development. Rural India is also badly in need of health care and education facilities, which would possibly reduce demographic pressures. In the urban areas, there is an urgent need to stimulate economic growth and to improve the functioning of urban labour markets. With rapid, widespread rural development resulting in rises in rural incomes, the market conditions for industrial development would be created. Part of the surplus from the rural areas flowing to the urban centres and the growing rural demand for manufactured goods would also pave the way for expansion of the formal sector. However, public investment to improve civic amenities, which are very poor indeed, would require greater policy attention.

It should be noted that the cheap credit that is available for production has few takers in the rural areas, mainly because of poor infrastructural support, and in the urban areas, mostly because of insufficient market demand and the poor availability of power. There are some who avail themselves of this cheap credit in spite of these constraints, but the large majority of them do not succeed and the resources are often wasted.

Overall, the results of this study indicate that migration raises the level of income of the poorer households. There is also some evidence that migration promotes the use of irrigation, leads to improvements in land and labour productivity and reduces under-employment in the rural areas. But the analysis shows that the lower the level of rural development in general and of infrastructural development in particular, the smaller the gains from migration. Moreover, the finding that many employed people migrate to the urban areas in search of better jobs and higher incomes, even when they have, at least initially, to face difficult urban labour market conditions, indicates that providing jobs in rural areas is not going to help much in retaining people unless differentials in income and living conditions are reduced between rural and urban areas. This can be achieved only if there is more rapid rural development and a clear cut migration policy, which is an essential component of an overall development strategy, linked and harmonized with policies on industrialization, agriculture and social welfare.

REFERENCES

Ahluwalia, I. J. 1985. *Industrial growth in India*. Oxford University Press, pp. 30–31.

Asha, Bhande; Tara Kanitkar. 1980. *Principle of population studies*. Himalaya Publishing House, Bombay.

Banerjee, Biswajit. 1986. *Rural to urban migration and the urban labour market*. Himalaya Publishing House, Delhi.

Government of India. Central Statistical Organization. 1984. *State Domestic Product*, Delhi.

———. Central Statistical Organization. 1984. *Statistical Abstract*, Delhi.

———. Central Statistical Organization. 1985. *Estimates of State Domestic Product*, Delhi

———. Central Statistical Organization. 1988. *Estimates of State Domestic Product*, Delhi.

———. Commission of Agricultural Costs and Prices. 1986. *Report on Prices for Kharif Crops, 1985–86 Season*, mimeo, Delhi.

———. Planning Commission. 1978. *Draft Five Year Plan, 1978-83*, Delhi.

———. Planning Commission. 1983. *Task forces on housing and urban development: I, Planning of urban development*, New Delhi.

———. Registrar General of India. 1983. *Census, 1981*, Paper 2, Delhi.

Joshi, Heather and Vijay. 1976. *Surplus labour and the city*, Oxford University Press, New Delhi.

Kannapan, S. 1983. *Employment problems and the urban labour market in developing nations*, East Lansing.

Makoto Kojima. 1981. 'Industrialization, income distribution and labour migration: The case of India', paper presented at the VIIIth World Economic Congress, 1–5 December, New Delhi.

Mohan, Rakesh. 1985. 'Urbanization in India's future', in *Population and Development Review*, 11, No. 4., December, pp. 634–35.

National Institute of Urban Affairs. 1988. *State of India's urbanization*, New Delhi.

Oberai, A. S.; H. K. Manmohan Singh. 1983. *Causes and consequences of internal migration: A study in the Indian Punjab*. Oxford University Press, New Delhi.

Prasad, Pradhan H. 1986. 'Institutional reforms and agricultural growth', in *Social Scientist*, June, pp. 3–19.

————. 1987. 'Agrarian violence in Bihar', in *Economic and Political Weekly*, 30 May, pp. 847–49.

Sen, Amartya Kumar. 1962. 'An aspect of Indian agriculture', in *Economic Weekly*, Annual Number, February.

Skeldon, R. 1986. 'On migration patterns in India during the 1970s', in *Population and Development Review*, 12(4), pp. 759–779.

Todaro, M. P. 1969. 'A model of labour migration and urban unemployment in less developed countries', in *American Economic Review*, Vol. 59, No. 1.

————. 1976. *Internal migration in developing countries*, Geneva, ILO.

United Nations. 1985. *World population trends, population and development interrelations and population policies: 1983 monitoring report*, Vols. I and II. New York.

————. 1987. *The prospects of world urbanisation*, Department of International Economic and Social Affairs, New York, table 2, p. 8.

Visaria, P.; Kothari, D. 1985. *Data base for the study of migration and urbanisation in India: A critical analysis*, Gujarat Institute of Area Planning, Working Paper No. 2, Ahmedabad.

INDEX